FORTH

Macmillan Computer Science Series

Consulting Editor
Professor F. H. Sumner, University of Manchester

S. T. Allworth, *Introduction to Real-time Software Design*
Ian O. Angell, *A Practical Introduction to Computer Graphics*
R. E. Berry and B. A. E. Meekings, *A Book on C*
G. M. Birtwistle, *Discrete Event Modelling on Simula*
T. B. Boffey, *Graph Theory in Operations Research*
Richard Bornat, *Understanding and Writing Compilers*
J. K. Buckle, *The ICL 2900 Series*
J. K. Buckle, *Software Configuration Management*
J. C. Cluley, *Interfacing to Microprocessors*
Robert Cole, *Computer Communications*
Derek Coleman, *A Structured Programming Approach to Data**
Andrew J. T. Colin, *Fundamentals of Computer Science*
Andrew J. T. Colin, *Programming and Problem-solving in Algol 68**
S. M. Deen, *Fundamentals of Data Base Systems**
P. M. Dew and K. R. James, *Introduction to Numerical Computation in Pascal*
K. C. E. Gee, *Introduction to Local Area Computer Networks*
J. B. Gosling, *Design of Arithmetic Units for Digital Computers*
David Hopkin and Barbara Moss, *Automata**
Roger Hutty, *Fortran for Students*
Roger Hutty, *Z80 Assembly Language Programming for Students*
Roland N. Ibbett, *The Architecture of High Performance Computers*
H. Kopetz, *Software Reliability*
E. V. Krishnamurthy, *Introductory Theory of Computer Science*
Graham Lee, *From Hardware to Software: an introduction to computers*
A. M. Lister, *Fundamentals of Operating Systems, third edition**
G. P. McKeown and V. J. Rayward-Smith, *Mathematics for Computing*
Brian Meek, *Fortran, PL/1 and the Algols*
Derrick Morris, *An Introduction to System Programming – Based on the PDP11*
Derrick Morris and Roland N. Ibbett, *The MU5 Computer System*
C. Queinnec, *LISP*
John Race, *Case Studies in Systems Analysis*
W. P. Salman, O. Tisserand and B. Toulout, *FORTH*
L. E. Scales, *Introduction to Non-Linear Optimization*
Colin J. Theaker and Graham R. Brookes, *A Practical Course on Operating Systems*
M. J. Usher, *Information Theory for Information Technologists*
B. S. Walker, *Understanding Microprocessors*
Peter J. L. Wallis, *Portable Programming*
I. R. Wilson and A. M. Addyman, *A Practical Introduction to Pascal – with BS 6192, second edition*

*The titles marked with an asterisk were prepared during the Consulting Editorship of Professor J. S. Rohl, University of Western Aurstralia.

FORTH

W. P. Salman

O. Tisserand and B. Toulout

MACMILLAN

Authorised English Language edition of
FORTH by W. P. Salman, O. Tisserand
and B. Toulout, first published 1983 by
Editions EYROLLES, 61 boulevard Saint-Germain,
75005 Paris

Translated by M. J. Stewart

First published 1984 by
Higher and Further Education Division
MACMILLAN PUBLISHERS LTD
Companies and representatives
throughout the world

Printed and bound in Great Britain at
The Camelot Press Ltd, Southampton

ISBN 0–333–36798-7

Contents

Preface

FORTH is a computer programming language that is sufficiently new to be unknown to the majority of those working in or studying computing. It challenges a number of received ideas about programming and leads to a more rigorous approach to problems.

In contrast to the standard languages, it is not restricted by a finite list of instructions and data structures. The user has the power to create his own language and tailor it to the required application.

All the programming work consists in adding new words to a vocabulary that is initially impersonal, but only using in each new definition words that are already known to the machine.

This type of programming lends itself particularly well to systematic testing methods and therefore increases the reliability of the programs produced.

Two other important features of this language are its speed and compactness. It is twenty to thirty-times faster than a normal BASIC, while still retaining the advantages of an interpreted language, and it can be more compact than assembler.

All these qualities make it a language that promises to enjoy a brilliant future in industry, because it allows the development costs of software to be reduced significantly, while ensuring increased reliability, and without being limited in its range of applications.

The purpose of this book is not only to enable you to use FORTH but also to show you its internal workings, since it is a language on the human scale.

The first chapter puts the language in context in the world of computing. Chapter 2 presents all the basic concepts of the language and makes the reader familiar with the dictionary, vocabularies, reverse Polish notation and the use of stacks.

In the third chapter, we go into the technical side of programming where you will see how to define words and execute them, using all the control structures that are provided for you in basic FORTH.

The purpose of chapter 4 is to introduce two standard vocabularies, the editor and the assembler.

Chapter 5 explains the mechanics of threaded languages. This chapter presupposes some knowledge of FORTH, since reference is frequently made to the language itself. A good knowledge of how such languages function leads to better quality programming and optimised use of the available tools.

Chapter 6 presents all the high-level tools that FORTH provides. It includes examples of the application of these high-level words for the definition of new data structures suitable for problem solving and new control structures.

In chapter 7 we take a closer look at some aspects of FORTH, namely vocabularies, segmentation, recursion and multitasking.

The eighth and final chapter contains a collection of problems, treated as worked examples and including commentary.

Included at the end of each chapter is a summary in tabular form of all the new words; several chapters also conclude with a selection of simple exercises, intended to provide immediate practice in the new concepts learned.

Both the authors and the publishers are especially grateful to Dick de Grandis Harrison for his assistance in the preparation of this English-language edition.

Thanks are also due to Jean Wild for typing the text.

1 Introduction and General Overview

1.1 HISTORICAL BACKGROUND

FORTH is the work of one man, Charles H. Moore. Its first complete implementation was on an IBM 1130, a third generation machine of the late 1960s.

Moore was sufficiently satisfied with the results of his work to want to call it the fourth generation language - FOURTH. However, unfortunately the IBM 1130 would only accept program names with five characters - hence the name FORTH.

After several parts of FORTH had been tested on different machines (Burroughs 5500, IBM 360) and in different languages (Algol, COBOL), FORTH was coded in FORTRAN, then in assembler, and then in FORTH.

The first application of FORTH was the programming of an IBM 2250 graphics terminal connected to an IBM 1130. A 32K FORTRAN program enabled simple diagrams to be drawn, whereas an 8K FORTH program provided three-dimensional moving graphics!

The first professional application of FORTH carried out by Charles Moore in 1971 on a Honeywell 316 was concerned with a problem in the acquisition of astronomical data at the National Radio Astronomy Observatory. This application was rerun at the NRAO Kitt Peak (Tucson) observatory on a PDP 11. During the past ten years this millimetre-wave radio telescope has enabled half the known interstellar molecules to be discovered.

In 1973 Charles Moore founded his company for the development of FORTH programs - FORTH Inc.

Because of the limitations of the astronomy market, other applications were quickly perfected. These included

MiniFORTH for minicomputers
Multiprogramming in FORTH
Data base management system in FORTH
PolyFORTH - a 'super' FORTH
MicroFORTH - a FORTH for microcomputers

In 1976, a committee of the International Astronomical Union adopted FORTH as the standard programming language for astronomy.

The number of people skilled in FORTH throughout the computing world is increasing from day to day. This has led to the creation of a FORTH Interest Group in the USA whose aim is to increase knowledge of the language. This group distributes the standard for the language chosen by the International FORTH Standard Team (the last standard dates from 1979).

This standard has been used as the core of the majority of the commercial versions of FORTH offered and simplifies program portability.

In the software industry, a new language will have no chance of being adopted unless it offers real solutions to the problems of software costs and reliability (in the broadest sense). Experience has shown that aesthetics is not a criterion of choice.

The headlong development of microcomputing and the continuing fall in component production costs cause manufacturers to wish to incorporate modern, efficient and user-friendly software at the lowest possible cost.

Currently, Pascal meets these requirements, but requires a quite complex configuration (48K plus mass storage) beyond the reach of most people.

In the professional field, computers are expected to solve problems that are often very complex. The programming languages used up until now impose such developmental and testing costs that software planning and investment can be questioned.

To predict the future of a new programming language, one must not simply pass judgement on the technical aspects, one most look at it in market terms. From the evolution of FORTH in recent years, everything leads one to think that it is solving efficiently the problems of its current users, whose numbers continue to increase.

As for the manufacturers, they are increasingly adopting FORTH as a base language on their machines. Some machines, like the Jupiter Ace, have even been designed for FORTH. In some fields of activity, such as games, astronomy, etc, FORTH has become the preferred development tool.

FORTH does not belong to the traditional language philosophy; it is therefore interesting to compare its characteristics with those of the traditional languages.

1.2 FORTH AND THE TRADITIONAL COMPUTING LANGUAGES

A computer language is only a tool like any other, and it must therefore be functional.

A good tool must be easy to use. For example, the great success of BASIC comes from the fact that no theoretical knowledge is required.

Our aim in this book is to show that anyone can learn FORTH, because the syntax is simple and non-restrictive, and because the user defines his own mnemonics and therefore chooses his own vocabulary for his dialogue with the machine.

During the development of an application it is useful to have permanent control of the syntax; this is the justification for the interpreter. But this facility must be paid for at the cost of execution speed. The ideal would be to have the execution speed of a compiled language and the help in development of an interpreter.

FORTH possesses both of these qualities by being a semi-compiled language.

Most high-level languages do not offer a data manipulation tool at the level of the memory bit. This is one of the reasons why external modules have to be written in assembler. Although a high-level language, standard FORTH allows such data manipulations. It can include a specialised ASSEMBLER vocabulary which allows assembler mnemonics to be used while remaining in FORTH. Some machines allow calls to be made to assembler routines from a program written in a high-level language, but these routines must be developed separately and must be resident in memory at the moment that they are called.

The characteristic feature in the generation of a high-level computer language is whether or not it is structured. Control structures are essential for clear programming. Paradoxically, this is the great shortcoming of the most widespread languages, such as COBOL, FORTRAN and BASIC.

As with Pascal, FORTH offers the standard control structures like BEGIN---WHILE---REPEAT. It even goes much further since it allows the user to create his own control and data structures.

One cannot overemphasise the importance of data structures in programming. Only good problem analysis can isolate from a mass of loose data the characteristics of structures and of the control of such structures.

The traditional languages offer the programmer no more than a fixed list of possible data structures and his problem is to make the least bad choice in order to approximate to the natural structures that emerge from his analysis.

The classic mistake of many an analyst is to reason from the point of view of his working language and not be able to extract the natural structures.

The conflict between data structures and language has of course been temporarily reduced by the appearance of data base management systems. They allow complex data structures to be supported, but are generally autonomous. Added to which, the interfaces with languages, when they do exist, are very difficult to manage and the programmer has to spend more time preparing and controlling access than actually processing the data.

In FORTH, the natural data structures resulting from an analysis, whatever they may be, can be embedded directly and the programmer can build for himself all the modes of access and control to the extent that he feels necessary.

FORTH is an adult language; it does not impose on the user a list of controls that experience has shown was inadequate from the start. It lets the programmer be the sole judge and guardian of the level of security to be applied to the software. It is in fact possible to create applications that are totally secure.

1.3 FORTH AND THE EXISTING MACHINES

However bizarre the concept may appear to the non-initiated, FORTH can be almost completely written in FORTH. Because of the small size of the active core that has to be written in the native machine language (less than 100 lines of assembler, for example), anyone well versed in the FORTH philosophy will be able to develop a FORTH standard on his own.

His method of working and the problems that he will have to solve are identical with those of all the applications that he may subsequently wish to develop in FORTH. There is no discontinuity between creation and use with FORTH. We hope that you will have caught the flavour of this new philosophy sufficiently to want to implement FORTH on your own preferred machine.

We shall now list some known implementations of FORTH, without making any claims that it is exhaustive. We have in fact just seen that implementation of the language is an easily solved problem, and quite within the capabilities of a single programmer. This in itself makes it impossible to chart the different implementations that have been made. Our only aim is to make you aware of the range of equipment that has been affected by this new philosophy.

Here are the implementations.

8-bit microprocessors
- Intel 8080, 8085, 8088
- Zilog Z80
- Motorola 6800, 6809
- RCA 1802
- Rockwell 6502

16-bit microprocessors
- Intel 8086, IAPX 186, IAPX 286
- Zilog Z8000
- Motorola 68000
- Digital Equipment LSI11
- Texas Instruments 9900

Microcomputers
- Apple II
- HP 85, HP 9826, HP 9836
- TRS 80
- Sinclair ZX81, ZX Spectrum
- Atari 800
- Commodore VIC 20
- Panasonic HHC
- Commodore PET
- IBM PC
- BBC Model B
- Heathkit 89/Zenith 89
- Northstar
- Cromenco
- Jupiter Ace
- SMS 300
- Goupil
- Commodore 64
- Dragon 32

Other computers
- PDP11, PDP10, PDP8
- NOVA
- HP 2100
- Burroughs 5500
- IBM 360, IBM 1130 Series 1
- Univac 1108
- Mod-Comp II
- CDC 6400
- Interdata
- Illiac
- Honeywell 316, Mini 6
- Varian 620
- GA SPC-16
- Phase IV
- Computer Automation LSI 4

1.4 SOME APPLICATIONS

FORTH is used extensively in producing special effects for films. For example, Elican Inc of Brea, California now uses FORTH to control camera systems of the type used to produce the film *Star Wars*. Such a system was also used by New World Productions of Venice, California, in making the film *Battle Beyond the Stars*. Similarly, Magican Inc, the company that produced the special effects for *Star Trek*, is now equipped with FORTH.

Remaining in the field of entertainment applications, we should mention the experience of the Atari company that developed a system of tests for arcade games using FORTH on a 6502 microprocessor. New arcade games now appearing on the market function in FORTH. Atari are also developing their home TV games in FORTH and already offer a version of FORTH called GameFORTH for their Atari 800 home computer.

The famous Los Angeles hospital, Cedar Sinai Medical Center, uses FORTH on a PDP11/60 to carry out the following tasks simultaneously

a) control 32 terminals
b) acquire data on patients by means of an optical reader and class it in an important data bank
c) carry out statistical operations on this data bank
d) carry out real-time blood analysis and cardiac analysis.

In addition, this hospital is currently developing a portable patient surveillance system, using a 6800 microprocessor, again all in FORTH.

The Craig M100 pocket translator, for translating between some twenty languages, depending on the chosen module, was developed in FORTH.

In the field of aerospace, we can mention two more applications, in addition to the radio telescopes to which we have already referred.

A special version of FORTH, called IPS, is used in an amateur radio satellite - OSCAR Phase III.

The company Avco Inc uses FORTH on an 1802 to monitor temperatures on a military satellite, as well as for telemetric data exchange.

Again, this list is by no means exhaustive. It only serves to show the diversity of the applications of FORTH, for management, process control, scientific calculation, and so on.

2 The FORTH Language

2.1 PREAMBLE

Before we begin to examine FORTH, let us consider the following three hypothetical programmers. First Mr X, who is interested in data processing using micros, has just acquired a personal microcomputer, and is using a programming language such as BASIC for the first time.

It is very probable that Mr X's first efforts in producing software will result in labyrinthine programs, involving solid blocks of tangled code. Mr X will quickly appreciate that his instinctive method of programming is not suited to complex problems, and can only produce programs of limited application, since any subsequent attempt to rework them only proves more time-consuming than starting from scratch.

It is clear that where Mr X went wrong was in improvising when faced with unforeseen problems rather than beginning with a thorough top-down analysis.

That is not to say that Mr X is entirely responsible for his haphazard approach. The traditional programming languages encourage piecemeal treatment, resorting to branching as the universal solution to the inevitable bad surprises that result from an inadequate initial analysis of the problem.

In contrast, Mr Y has much greater experience of programming. He has already learnt to overcome the problems that Mr X ran into and has evolved a method of dealing with them.

He analyses the problems thoroughly, identifies the data structures, and divides up his programming into separate blocks. He can then link these blocks together using the control structures that are available to him.

He has less difficulty in perfecting his program and documenting his work. However, every new problem requires him to begin at the beginning. He knows how to identify blocks, but does not know how to build modules of general applicability that can be reused in different programs.

Development times remain long, because he does not know how to adopt a global approach to problems and provide himself with reusable tools.

As for Mr Z, he has long outgrown the situations of both X and Y, although through laziness he makes no effort at careful programming. His strength and efficiency lie in the fact that he knows how to generalise his procedures so that he can reuse them easily and confidently when new problems have to be analysed.

Nonetheless, he suffers from not being able to integrate these procedures into the language library, so that they can be even more readily available for use.

His ideal would be to be able to extend his working language according to the requirements of the application.

We hope to show in the remainder of this book how FORTH could be of great value to X, Y and Z.

2.2 FIRST CONTACT

2.2.1 The Concept of the Word

Up until now the programmer has had to subject himself to the limitations of the communicating language when writing programs. With FORTH, the programmer can teach his language to the machine; thus a dialogue is set up.

A conventional program consists of a string of catalogued instructions. In FORTH, dialogue with the machine is achieved by communicating sequences of words. The user can decide to give a name to any sequence of words, and from that point the machine will recognise that sequence as a new word of the language.

It goes without saying that FORTH already recognises an important list of words that carry out both simple and complicated tasks.

The concept of a program, and that of an instruction, no longer exist. The programming task consists in constructing or extending a vocabulary by defining new words from words already known to the machine.

2.2.2 The Concept of the Dictionary

Like a human being, the machine has a dictionary that it expands by learning new words.

As in all languages, a dictionary is a shapeless and bulky object. It is natural to organise it into vocabularies of words having common characteristics, that are free and subjective. To convince yourself of this, try extracting quickly from a twenty-volume encyclopedia all the words relating to information technology.

FORTH offers the possibility of reasoning in terms of vocabularies.

When the machine is presented with a word, it goes to find out whether it already knows that word by exploring the vocabulary that you have selected for it.

Of course, all apprenticeship is based on acquired knowledge, which means that in order to teach your machine a new word you may only use words that it already knows from its everyday vocabulary.

Once the apprenticeship has finished, the machine then has a definition of the new word to which it can refer.

Stretching the meaning of the word definition, we shall also use it to describe this apprenticeship phase.

Of course, you may well change your mind and redefine an existing word. When FORTH needs to recognise a word, it will always refer to the most recent definition that it knows.

Every new definition of a word will not be taken account of by words that related to the previous definition of that word.

Example

The word POLITENESS is defined with the help of the word GOOD-DAY.
The word GREETING is defined with the help of the word POLITENESS.

GREETING therefore indirectly uses the word GOOD-DAY.

If the word POLITENESS is redefined with the word GOOD-BYE, the word GREETING will still continue to use the old version of POLITENESS, and therefore the word GOOD-DAY.

We have been at pains to indicate straight away what might appear to be a first obstacle for the beginner in FORTH, as a result of his traditional computer education. But we shall see that not only is this problem quite solvable, but the FORTH philosophy can even gain advantage from it.

Initiation
Among its base words, FORTH contains the word FORGET which makes it possible to delete previously defined words.

Example
Suppose that the words HOUR, MINUTE and SECOND were the last to be defined, in that order.

The syntax

```
FORGET HOUR <Return> OK
```

will delete the word HOUR from the dictionary, as well as all the words defined after HOUR, that is the words MINUTE and SECOND.

It is always the last definition of the word that follows FORGET that will be taken into account.

So if we define successively HOUR, MINUTE, SECOND, then define HOUR again

```
FORGET HOUR <Return> OK
```

only deletes the last definition of HOUR.

2.2.3 Definition of a Word
In FORTH all words must be separated by a (white) space. This is the only separator.

Every simple definition of a word begins with the word {:} (signalling the start of the learning process), followed by the name of the word being defined and ending with the word {;} (signalling the end of the learning process). *Note* In the text, wherever a FORTH word might be confused with a punctuation mark, it is enclosed within curly brackets.

Example
Referring to our previous example, we can write

```
: POLITENESS GOOD-DAY ; <Return> OK
: GREETING POLITENESS ; <Return> OK
```

The FORTH word {(} indicates that the text which follows is commentary; the end of the comment is marked with a closing bracket. Comments can appear at any time in the dialogue, including in the middle of a definition.

It will be noticed immediately that there is much freedom in the layout of text, thanks to the nature of the separator.

Example
The following two definitions are equivalent.

```
: TOTO TITI TATA ; <Return> OK
: TOTO     ( Definition of the word TOTO ) <Return>
  TITI     ( Action ... ) <Return>
  TATA     ( Action ... ) <Return>
; <Return> OK
```

2.2.4 FORTH Objects
In FORTH, the data manipulated can be variables, constants or pre-

defined constants. Note that these objects are of a different nature within the machine itself. Thus the value of a constant is not immediately modifiable.

To declare and initialise a variable, the syntax is as follows

value VARIABLE name of variable

For constants the syntax is similar

value CONSTANT name of constant

Immediate constants are volatile numerical values.

We shall examine the manipulation of these objects later. We would only point out at this stage that FORTH is in no sense constrained by data structures. We shall explain how quickly and easily we can begin to define structures such as character strings, and matrices, as well as personalised structures.

2.2.5 Structure of the LIFO Stack

FORTH is built around two stacks. One is the data stack; the other is the return stack.

We frequently come across the concept of the stack in daily life. So a stack of plates that is only added to at the top represents a structure in which the first plate put in position will be the last to be removed and conversely the last positioned will be the first to be removed.

It is precisely this latter characteristic - Last In First Out - which defines the data structure called the LIFO stack.

Although transparent for the user, this structure is used in the resolution of many basic computer functions, such as calculations of arithmetic expressions, calls to subprograms, syntactical analysis, and so on.

Setting up a stack structure in a machine is done in the following way. The data are stored sequentially from a given address which is held in a special register. Additions and subtractions are made by referring to another address specified in a second special register which continually provides the first available cell. This register is the stack pointer.

These two registers are initialised to the same value. The equality condition will always correspond to an empty stack. It is easy to control its expansion by fixing its capacity in a third special register. The equality condition between the stack pointer and this third register will correspond to a full stack.

The user can very easily manually place data on the data stack or remove them. For example, the word {.} (Dot) removes the top of the stack and displays it on the screen.

So, you could execute

```
12 <Return> OK
24 <Return> OK
33 <Return> OK
```

Followed by

```
. <Return> 33 OK
. <Return> 24 OK
. <Return> 12 OK
```

Here the data have been displayed in the inverse order of their introduction.

Execution of a further {.} will prompt an error message to indicate that the data stack is empty.

All the above is quite logical. But how does one explain the fact that the interpreter accepted the words 12, 24 and 33 which have never been defined?

Let us look again at the mechanics of the interpreter.

The interpreter is activated as soon as you touch the <Return> key; it analyses the contents of your sentence. The words are easily identified thanks to the space separator. Each word first prompts a search in the dictionary. If the word is found, the machine carries out the necessary function.

In our example above, 12 does not appear in the dictionary. The interpreter will therefore try to identify it as a predefined constant, that is a number expressed in the current base. Note in fact that FORTH can work to any base, as we shall see later. If the number is valid, it will be placed at the top of the stack; if not, an error message will appear.

2.2.6 Reverse Polish Notation

Introduction

When you use your pocket calculator, the operations are directly executed in order and progressively as the data are entered.

Thus

    1 + 2 * 3

will produce 9

If you want it to calculate 1 + (2*3), you will have to rearrange your order of entry and key

    2 * 3 + 1   which will give 7 this time

It is therefore the order of entry that governs the result of the calculation, all the operators being made common-place.

In a computer the methodology is different. It only interprets your commands on receipt of an end signal, for example the act of pressing the <Return> key. It then analyses the expression and can execute it in a non-sequential order.

If we type in A+B*C, most languages will first evaluate B*C, then add A. They have in fact been 'taught' a hierarchy of operators. The traditional order for operators is as follows

    ↑(power), - (negation), * and /, + and -, ...

The left to right sequential order in the expression decides the priority for operators at the same level.

This hierarchy present a problem if we want an operator of lower priority to be executed first. For example, if in A+B*C we wanted to add A and B first, then multiply the result by C, we should have to introduce the delimiters (and).

We should have to write (A+B)*C.

The automatic recognition system is therefore more elaborate, and the manipulations become more complex.

Polish notation

Imagine a notation that does not modify the order of operands and whose execution is always carried out from left to right. This left→right direction is an arbitrary choice.

Such a notation would allow removal of hierarchies and therefore parentheses; it would also limit the automatic process to the simple recognition of operands and operators.

The system of execution would then be as follows

a) all operands are stored as they are encountered

b) the operators are executed immediately. They operate on the last two operands stored, the latter being then destroyed, and the result is stored in memory like a new operand.

This method of managing operands fits in perfectly with the structure of the LIFO stack already described.

Note that all the traditional arithmetic interpreters always put expressions into this form before executing them.

It is conventional to use ↑ to indicate placing on the stack and ↓ to indicate removal from the stack.

Examples

A+B, written A B + will be executed as follows

```
A:↑
B:↑
+:↓↓(A+B)↑
```

(A+B)*C, written A B + C * will be executed as

```
A:↑
B:↑
+:↓↓(A+B)↑
C:↑
*:↓↓(A+B)*C↑
```

A+B*C, written A B C * + will be executed as

```
A:↑
B:↑
C:↑
*:↓↓(B*C)↑
+:↓↓A+(B*C)↑
```

It will be seen that there is always one more addition to the stack than there is a removal from it. This is because the final result remains on the stack.

Arithmetic operations

At your FORTH terminal you can immediately apply the concepts presented above.

Type

1 2 + <Return> <u>OK</u>

Then, to display the result

. <Return> <u>OK</u>

Do not forget that all the arithmetic operators are FORTH words just like any others. From now on therefore we shall only speak of arithmetic words. When used, these will seek out their operands in the stack and store their results there.

2.2.7 Conventions in Notation

Dialogue with the machine

All the control keys are enclosed within less-than and greater-than signs, for example

<Return> <Ctl> <Esc> <Break> <Shift>

All the machine responses are underlined. In addition, FORTH hands back control to the user by displaying OK.

Stack representation

The stack is shown between brackets, showing from left to right the data in order of entry, followed by ---.

For example, after carrying out the following

```
1 <Return> OK
2 <Return> OK
```

The stack will appear as follows

```
( 1 2 --- )
```

Representation of the action of FORTH words on the stack

Paremeters on the stack that are used by a word are shown in brackets. They are listed with the top of the stack to the right, and are separated by --- from those returned after execution.

Example

```
+  ( n1 n2 --- n2+n2 )
.  ( n --- )
```

2.2.8 Semi-compilation

Interpreted approach

In interpreted mode, the program lines are analysed immediately. Once recognised, the key words are replaced by their codes (tokens).

On execution, when one of these tokens is encountered, the program looks it up in a table which will give it the corresponding executable code address.

Compiled approach

The user first edits the text of his program in an editor. He then calls the compiler which carries out a global analysis of the text, replacing the key words with machine language that can be directly executed.

Semi-compiled approach

The programmer converses line by line with the interpreter. The latter replaces the key words, not with tokens, but directly with the execution address of the appropriate key word.

This approach brings together the advantages of the previous two - program flexibility and speed of execution.

Semi-compilation exists in most languages. However, since these languages have a fixed library of key words, the programs are necessarily verbose, and the user only has a finite range of tools available to him.

With FORTH, the extensibility of the language allows one to define words of optimum size and semi-compilation can then demonstrate its power.

2.3 THE FORTH VOCABULARY

Like any vocabulary, the FORTH vocabulary contains the list of FORTH words. There is no classification according to any special sorting criterion, the words are simply stored in their chronological order of creation.

The dictionary, which comprises all the vocabularies, has the traditional form of a linked list.

Each word is represented by its name, a series of pointers and its semi-compiled definition.

Then there is the link pointer which enables a word to be looked up in the vocabulary. It contains the address of the word preceding any word in the list. For the first word defined this pointer contains zero.

It is equally necessary to store the address of the last word created. This is the starting point of every search back towards the first word defined.

Example

The word VLIST allows you to obtain the complete list of words in the working vocabulary, that is, the FORTH at that moment. The nature of the chaining means that the words appear in inverse chronological order.

2.4 MODULARITY OF THE LANGUAGE

One of the interesting features of FORTH is that the base dictionary is modular. The user can begin to work with a very restricted vocabulary. Depending on his needs, he can at any time call specialised FORTH modules.

The modules that exist on the main versions of FORTH are the following

- double-length working (32 bits)
- floating point calculation
- mathematical and graphical functions
- printer control
- virtual memory and editor control
- assemblers
- input/output control

These frameworks allow the user to optimise the vocabulary according to the application, with the associated benefits of less demand on storage capacity and a reduction in vocabulary search time and interpretation time.

2.5 GENERALISATION OF THE VOCABULARY CONCEPT

Up until now, we have presented the role of the programmer as to define new words in the FORTH vocabulary.

But there is the further possibility of creating new vocabularies. It is in fact possible to work in vocabularies with different contexts, which are specific for each application.

This general structure of vocabularies has many ramifications, but it remains transparent to the user. At any given moment, the machine only knows the context of the vocabulary in which the user finds himself. Figure 2.1 illustrates this structure.

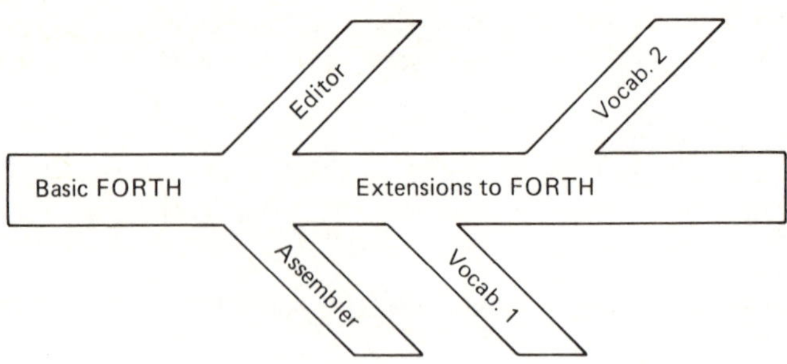

Figure 2.1

The set of words that belongs to the different vocabularies constitutes the FORTH dictionary. We shall see later how the user can create his own vocabularies.

The traditional implementations of FORTH include three vocabularies: FORTH, EDITOR, ASSEMBLER.

To transfer from one vocabulary to another, one has simply to type the name of the vocabulary required.

Example

EDITOR <Return> OK
FORTH <Return> OK

2.6 SUMMARY

Word	*Syntax*	*Definition*
FORGET	FORGET "name"	Deletes from the dictionary all defined words back to and including "name".
:	: "name" "definition" ;	Word indicating that the user defines a new word. The beginning word of a definition.
;	: "name" "definition" ;	Word indicating the end of a word definition. {;} can only be used with {:}.
(	("comment")	Word indicating that the following text is only commentary. Always used with).
)	("comment")	Word indicating the end of a comment.
VARIABLE	"initial value" VARIABLE "name" of variable"	Word defining a variable.
CONSTANT	"value" CONSTANT "name of constant"	Word defining a constant. The fundamental difference between a constant and a variable is that once defined the value of a constant cannot be altered.

.	. (n ---)	Unstacks a 16-bit signed value and displays it in the current base. The displayed value is no longer on the stack.
VLIST	VLIST	Displays on the screen the list of FORTH words that make up the context vocabulary.
FORTH	FORTH	Makes FORTH the context vocabulary.
EDITOR	EDITOR	Makes EDITOR the context vocabulary.
ASSEMBLER	ASSEMBLER	Makes ASSEMBLER the context vocabulary.

2.7 EXERCISES

2.1 What remains on the stack after the following sequences?

a) 1 2 3 . . 4 . . 5 .
b) 23 45 . 33 54 1 8 . .
c) 32 15 11 7 . .
d) 9 . 12 . 13 14 . 15 18

2.2 Translate the following expressions into reverse Polish notation.

a) (a+b)*(c+d)
b) ((a+b)/c)+((d+e)*f)
c) (a/(b+c))/((d+e)*(a/c))
d) (a*(b/c))+((d+a)*(b/(c+d)))

3 How to Program

3.1 OBJECTS AND THEIR MANIPULATION

3.1.1 Reading and Writing in Memory

FORTH works on 16-bit cells. To read the contents of a memory cell, all that is needed is to place the address of the required cell on the stack and execute the word {@} (Fetch), which returns the contents in the stack.

Example Read the contents of address 12588

12588 @ . <Return> 5163 OK

There is a FORTH word which causes the contents of a given cell to be shown directly on the screen. This is the word {?}.
In our example, one could therefore also type

12588 ? <Return> 5163 OK

It is customary to express memory addresses in base 16 (hexadecimal). In FORTH it is easy to change base by using the words HEX (→ 16) and DECIMAL (→ 10).

Example

12588 HEX . <Return> 312C OK

To write a 16-bit value in a memory cell, the principle is the same. The value followed by the address are placed in the stack; then the word {!} (Store) is executed.

Example Write 3F00 to address 312C

HEX 3F00 312C ! <Return> OK

It is possible to work on 8-bit cells (1 byte) using the words {C@} and {C!}.

Example Reread the contents of addresses 312C and 312D

312C C@ . <Return> 0 OK
312D C@ . <Return> 3F OK

It will be noticed that the word {!} presented above places the LSB (Least Significant Byte) at the specified address and the MSB (Most Significant Byte) at the next following address. This ordering may be different in other implementations.

3.1.2 Defining and Using Constants

We have already seen how to define and use a constant for the first time

Value CONSTANT Name

As soon as the constant has been defined, the function of the new FORTH word "Name" is to place the value of the constant on the data stack.

Thus

```
16 CONSTANT SIXTEEN <Return> OK
SIXTEEN . <Return> 16 OK
```

3.1.3 Defining and Using Variables

To define a variable, the same principle applies

```
Value   VARIABLE   Name
```

As soon as the variable has been defined, the function of the new FORTH word "Name", in this case, is to place the address of the value on the stack.

Thus

```
15 VARIABLE LENGTH <Return> OK
LENGTH <Return> OK          ( Address --- )
@ <Return> OK               ( Value --- )
. <Return> OK               ( --- )
```

Expressed in other terms

```
LENGTH ? <Return> 15 OK
```

To modify the value of a variable the word {!} introduced in 3.1.1 will of course be used.

Example

```
14 LENGTH ! <Return> OK
LENGTH ? <Return> 14 OK
```

3.1.4 User Variables

User variables are special FORTH variables used by the interpreter.

Example DP (the dictionary pointer) has as its value the address of the first free location in the dictionary.

BASE has as its value the current working numeric base.

In this context, the definition of {HEX} is

```
: HEX 16 BASE ! ; <Return> OK
```

To find out the current base, one only needs to type

```
BASE ? <Return> 10 OK
```

It will be noted that to display the current base in the current base is quite pointless, since the value will always be 10.

More seriously though, if we want to display the current base in decimal, without changing it, we can define the following word

```
: WHAT-BASE
    BASE @      ( Val-base --- )
    BASE @      ( Val-base Val-base --- )
    DECIMAL     ( Val-base Val-base --- )
    .           ( Val-base --- )
    BASE        ( Val-base Ad-base --- )
    !           ( --- )
; <Return> OK
```

The following can then be executed

HEX WHAT-BASE <Return> 16 OK

3.2 STACKS AND THEIR MANIPULATION

3.2.1 The Data Stack

Since this stack has already been introduced in detail, we shall now describe the manipulation tools connected with it.

When introducing the word {.} we saw that its execution systematically destroyed the top of the stack. How therefore can we consult the top of the stack without destroying it? The answer is to begin by duplicating it, by using the word DUP.

Example

```
1 <Return> OK      ( 1 --- )
DUP <Return> OK    ( 1 1 --- )
. <Return> 1 OK
```

There are four other important words

DROP (n ---) destroys the top of the stack
SWAP (n1 n2 --- n2 n1) swaps the last two items of data entered
OVER (n1 n2 --- n1 n2 n1) which duplicates the last but one item of data entered on the top of the stack
ROT (n1 n2 n3 --- n2 n3 n1) which carries out a circular permutation on the last three items of data.

All these manipulations apply to 16-bit data using a single cell in the stack.

However, each of these words has its equivalent for the manipulation of double cells. These are

```
2DUP    (n1 n2 --- n1 n2 n1 n2 )
2DROP   (n1 n2 --- )
2SWAP   (n1 n2 n3 n4 --- n3 n4 n1 n2 )
2OVER   (n1 n2 n3 n4 --- n1 n2 n3 n4 n1 n2 )
2ROT    (n1 n2 n3 n4 n5 n6 --- n3 n4 n5 n6 n1 n2 )
```

It will be noted that the majority of these words have an action different from that of the repetition of the corresponding words working on 16 bits.

Example

```
DUP DUP (n1 n2 --- n1 n2 n2 n2 )
2DUP    (n1 n2 --- n1 n2 n1 n2 )
```

3.2.2 The Return Stack

Like all high-level languages, FORTH uses a special LIFO stack to store the return addresses of the calling procedures. The essential difference is that FORTH gives the user access to this stack by means of the following two words

>R which transfers the cell at the top of the data stack to the top of the return stack.
R> which carries out the reverse operation.

This auxiliary stack is most frequently used for the temporary unloading of the data stack.

For example, the return stack can be conveniently used to give the definition of the words 2DUP, 2DROP, 2SWAP, 2OVER and 2ROT, as follows

```
: 2DUP      OVER OVER ; <Return> OK
: 2DROP     DROP DROP ; <Return> OK
: 2SWAP     ROT >R ROT R> ; <Return> OK
: 2OVER     >R >R 2DUP R> R> 2SWAP ; <Return> OK
: 2ROT      >R >R 2SWAP R> R> 2SWAP ; <Return> OK
```

There are other, rarer uses of this stack. For example, try typing

```
: GOODNIGHT 123 >R ; <Return> OK
GOODNIGHT <Return>
```

If you have tried it, you will appreciate that this type of use is the preserve of experts.

In fact, you should never forget that the interpreter uses this stack constantly to store procedure return addresses. If you use it within a definition, you must remember to leave it in the same state as you found it.

3.3 ARITHMETIC WORDS

3.3.1 Introduction

FORTH has special arithmetic words for each of the following types of data

single-length signed numbers (16 bits)
single-length unsigned numbers
double-length signed numbers (32 bits)
double-length unsigned numbers
floating numbers.

In addition, there are words for converting from one type to another, as well as words called mixed that work on several types at once.

It is customary to represent each of these types on the stack in the following way

n : signed single length
u : unsigned single length
d : signed double length
ud : unsigned double length
f : floating

Negative numbers are represented quite traditionally by their two's complement. The principle of this method of representation consists in complementing all the bits of the number, then adding 1 to the number thus obtained.

Example 12 is represented by 0000 0000 0000 1100
(in hexadecimal 0 0 0 C)

-12 is represented by 1111 1111 1111 0011
+0000 0000 0000 0001
1111 1111 1111 0100
(or in hexadecimal F F F 4)

It should be remembered that the value of the number held in a cell depends on the type that has been allocated to it. For example, suppose a cell contains the hexadecimal number FFF4. If this is taken to be signed, its value will be -12; if it is taken to be unsigned, its value will be 65524.

3.3.2 Single-length Words

FORTH of course has available the four basic words + - * /, which here operate on signed numbers. Here the word / represents integer division.

Example

```
13 5 / . <Return> 2 OK
```

The effect of these words on the stack is shown as follows

```
+   ( n1 n2 --- n1+n2 )
-   ( n1 n2 --- n1-n2 )
*   ( n1 n2 --- n1*n2 )
/   ( n1 n2 --- n1/n2 )
```

In order to obtain the remainder of the integer division, the word MOD is used; this works on unsigned numbers.

Example

```
13 5 MOD . <Return> 3 OK
MOD    ( u1 u2 --- u-remainder )
```

The word /MOD provides both the quotient and the remainder in an integer division.

Example

```
13 5 /MOD . . <Return> 2 3 OK

/MOD ( u1 u2 --- u-remainder u-quotient )
```

You can verify that /MOD could be defined using the words MOD and / in the following way

```
: /MOD 2DUP MOD ROT ROT / ; <Return> OK
```

Suppose now that you wish to calculate a percentage, for example 45% of 11241. You might be tempted to use one of the two following solutions

```
   11241 45 * 100 /
or 11241 100 / 45 *
```

The first solution would be rejected by the machine as being out of range, because the product 45*11241 will not fit 16 bits. You would therefore be compelled to use the second. However, the integer division would give a less accurate result. To compensate for this inconvenience, there is a FORTH word which links together the operations * and /, using an intermediate result in 32 bits. This is the word */.

```
*/  ( n1 n2 n3 --- n1*n2/n3 )
```

You will then have

```
11241 45 100 */
```

Here the division remains integer division, and there is therefore a word that provides both the quotient and the remainder at the same time, while respecting the constraints of */. This is the word */MOD.

```
*/MOD   ( u1 u2 u3 --- u-remainder u-quotient )
```

Example

```
11241 45 100 */MOD . . <Return> 5058 45 OK
```

Here now are four words whose usage is well known

```
ABS      ( n --- |n| )
NEGATE   ( n --- -n )
MIN      ( n1 n2 --- Min(n1,n2) )
MAX      ( n1 n2 --- Max(n1,n2) )
```

There is another family of arithmetic words, one of whose operands is fixed. Examples are 1+, 2+, 1-, 2*, and so on. Their use is self explanatory.

Example

```
5 2* . <Return> 10 OK
```

Their sole purpose is to reduce interpretation time. In practice, in establishing a definition one usually needs operations like 'add 1', 'subtract 2', etc. So, using the word 1+, for example, rather than the syntax 1 +, only requires one interpreter search and therefore speeds up the interpretation.

The most frequently defined words of this type are

```
1+  ( n --- n+1 )
1-  ( n --- n-1 )
2+  ( n --- n+2 )
2-  ( n --- n-2 )
2*  ( n --- n*2 )
2/  ( n --- n/2 )
```

In conclusion we should mention the word {U.} which, in contrast to the word {.} which displays the top of the stack as a signed value, displays this same value, but unsigned.

Example

```
-12 .  <Return> -12 OK
-12 U. <Return> 65524 OK
```

3.3.3 Double-length Words

Double-length addition and subtraction is effected by means of the words D+ and D-.

```
D+  ( d1 d2 --- d1+d2 )
D-  ( d1 d2 --- d1-d2 )
```

Similarly, there are the equivalents of NEGATE, ABS, MIN and MAX.

```
DNEGATE  ( d --- -d )
DABS     ( d --- |d| )
DMIN     ( d1 d2 --- Min(d1,d2) )
DMAX     ( d1 d2 --- Max(d1,d2) )
```

We need to have words that allow double-length input-outputs on the stack.

In order to introduce a double-length number into the stack, a special delimiter needs to be included in its expression; this is usually a full stop. Stacking always occurs in the order LSW, MSW.

Example

```
.12 <Return> OK
. <Return> 0 OK
. <Return> 12 OK
```

To display directly a double-length number located at the top of the stack, the word {D.} is used.

```
D.  ( d --- )
```

Example

```
.12 D.   <Return> 12 OK
12 0 D.  <Return> 12 OK
0 2 D.   <Return> 131072 OK
```

There is a type conversion word which converts a single-length signed number at the top of the stack into a double-length signed number.

```
S->D  ( n --- d )
```

Example

```
12 S->D.  <Return> 12 OK
```

3.3.4 Mixed-length Words

It may for example be practical to be able to add different length numbers without having to make a conversion. FORTH has the following words to help here.

```
M+     ( d n --- d-sum )
M/     ( d n --- n-quotient )(integer division )
U/MOD  ( ud u --- u-remainder u-quotient )
M*     ( n1 n2 --- d-product )
U*     ( u1 u2 --- ud-product )
M*/    ( d n u --- d-result )
```

In the same way that +/ used a double-length intermediate result, M*/ uses a triple-length intermediate result.

Try to familiarise yourself with these different words by using them on examples of your own choosing.

3.3.5 Fixed Point Versus Floating Point

As you will have no doubt noticed, up until now we have only introduced arithmetic words working on integers.

Fixed-point principle

In this number storage system, the program itself takes control of the point, which remains invisible to the machine.

For example, if you have to carry out management accounting calculations, you can express all the numbers in pence, thus carry out all the calculations with integers (single or double length), then only introduce the decimal point when printing out the results, that is if these need to be shown in pounds.

The numerical values are stored in fixed-length locations, and during the course of calculations there is the risk of overflow.

In double length, the range of numbers that can be represented therefore extends from -2 147 483 648 to +2 147 483 647.

One of the programmer's first tasks therefore is to establish the optimum scale factor, depending on the degree of precision required.

Thus, in the financial management context, all the numbers will probably be expressed in thousands of pounds.

At all levels, this is the most natural approach. This is illustrated by the following typical applications.

Real-time data acquisition

If you have examined a modern piece of measuring equipment, equipped with a display, you will have seen that the data are calibrated in such a way that the user can set the scale factor to appear in fixed format. Sometimes the decimal point is even marked on the actual panel - an indication of the fixed-point approach.

Let us now look at the more general case of the acquisition of data that always occurs in a real-time problem.

The intermediate device between a physical process and a calculator is composed of one or more sensors followed by an amplification and an analogue to digital conversion. The choice of the electronic amplifier converter even governs the range of values that will appear. The choice of scale for fixed-point calculations is therefore directly dictated by this interface device.

Management

One of the analytical stages of a traditional management application consists of an in-depth dissection of all the data. The length of the alphanumeric data is fixed, as are the maximum and minimum values of all the numerical data.

This is the preparatory work for a fixed-point calculation. Fixed-point working, which is often quite possible, is the best choice because, for purely technical reasons that we shall explain later, it allows the calculation time to be cut by more than a third.

Floating-point principle

If fixed point is used clumsily, the problem of overflow occurs all too frequently. In general, the programmer would like to be able to leave it to the machine to take care of scale changes automatically; for example in multiplications.

Working in floating point makes this possible.

The data are expressed in the machine in the following form

Sign	Exponent	Mantissa

where the exponent is calculated so that the mantissa fits in to the left.

This automatic handling of changes in scale by the machine has certainly been ill thought through and can be held to be detrimental to good programming.

What are the legitimate uses of the floating point?

1. You want to use the machine as a floating-point calculator.
2. You value development time more highly than execution time.
3. The variation in range of your data is really too great.
4. You have a hard-wired, floating-point processor which optimises this type of calculation.

For its part, FORTH has many more affinities for fixed point than for floating point, since it fits in better with the moderate and precise character of the FORTH programmer.

It should be remembered that, however convenient for the programmer, a floating-point calculation causes the machine to have to carry out a great many more operations than an equivalent fixed-point calculation. Execution times are the first to suffer.

Let us for example compare a multiplication calculation.

In fixed point, this comes down to the traditional algorithm of shift addition.

In floating point, the machine will first have to add the exponents, then multiply the mantissas, then recalculate the exponent so that the mantissa is normalised.

During the calculation, memory use is no longer optimised, since the exponents and mantissas must be handled in parallel.

On the other hand, in fixed point the machine only has to contend with integers with which it can calculate very quickly.

This bias in FORTH towards fixed point is so pronounced that the early versions of FORTH did not provide for floating-point calculations; these were introduced later in the form of modules, as we have already described.

3.4 COMPARISON WORDS

3.4.1 Boolean Variables

As in many high-level languages, boolean variables are not physically different from other variables. The condition FALSE corresponds to a null value, all the other values corresponding to a TRUE condition.

The comparison words function in the following way. The parameters are first stored on the stack, and the result of the comparison will be returned to the stack as a single-precision boolean variable.

```
( var1 var2 --- flag )
```

In what follows, we shall indicate the boolean parameters on the stack by the symbol b.

3.4.2 Single-length Comparisons

FORTH contains the following list of comparison words

```
=    ( n1 n2 --- b )    tests if n1=n2
U<   ( u1 u2 --- b )    tests if u1<u2
<    ( n1 n2 --- b )    tests if n1<n2
>    ( n1 n2 --- b )    tests if n1>n2
0=   ( n --- b )        tests if n=0
0>   ( n --- b )        tests if n>0
0<   ( n --- b )        tests if n<0
```

Note When comparing numbers greater than 32767, this fact has to be communicated to the interpreter, so that it does not take them to be signed numbers. To appreciate this fully, try the following

```
6000 A000 < . <Return> 0 OK
6000 A000 U< . <Return> 1 OK
```

Think about this.

3.4.3 Double-length Comparisons

The following words belong to this category

```
D=    ( d1 d2 --- b )     tests if ( d1=d2 )
D<    ( d1 d2 --- b )     tests if ( d1<d2 )
DU<   ( ud1 ud2 --- b )   tests if ( ud1<ud2 ) in 32 bits
```

3.4.4 Boolean Operators

The traditionally used boolean operators are AND, OR and complement - represented in FORTH respectively by *, +, and 0=.

For memory, the truth tables of these three logical operators are

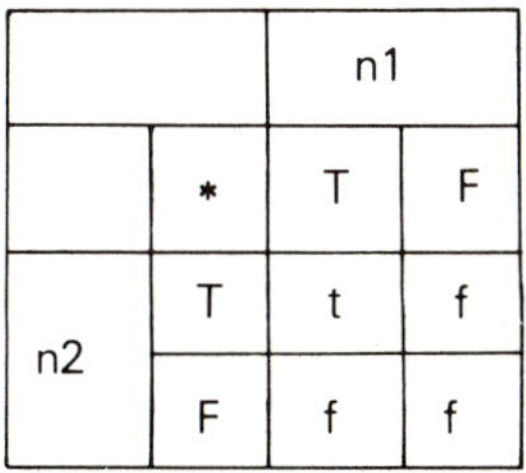

		n1	
	*	T	F
n2	T	t	f
	F	f	f

AND

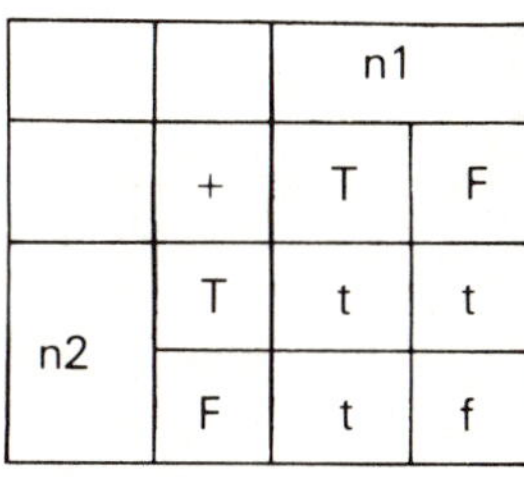

		n1	
	+	T	F
n2	T	t	t
	F	t	f

OR

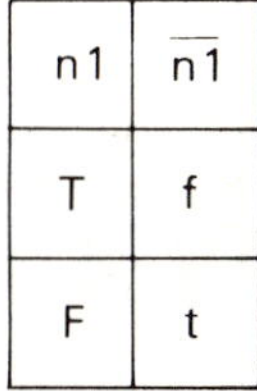

n1	$\overline{n1}$
T	f
F	t

Complement

Let us take as an application example a test to establish if a number belongs to an open interval.

The values will be entered on the stack in the order

```
( Lower bound n Upper bound --- )
```

The result of the test is itself returned to the stack.

The test is very simply described as

```
( n Lower bound ) AND ( n Upper bound )
```

which in FORTH becomes

```
: INTERVAL      ( Lower bound n Upper bound --- )
          OVER  ( Lower bound n Upper bound n --- )
          >     ( Lower bound n b1 --- )
          >R    ( Lower bound n --- )
          <     ( b2 --- )
          R>    ( b2 b1 --- )
          *     ( b2 and b1 --- )
; <Return> OK
1 2 3 INTERVAL . <Return> 1 OK
```

Some languages contain the EXCLUSIVE OR whose truth table is

	n1		
	XOR	T	F
n2	T	f	t
	F	t	f

As an exercise, we shall define the word EXOR which fulfils this function. It can be seen that A XOR B is easily written

```
(A OR B) AND (Ā OR B̄)
: XOR                 ( n1 n2 --- )
           2DUP       ( n1 n2 n1 n2 --- )
           +          ( n1 n2 (n1 or n2) --- )
           >R         ( n1 n2 --- )
           0=         ( n1 n2 --- )
           SWAP       ( n2 n1 --- )
           0=         ( n̅2̅ n̅1̅ --- )
           +          ( (n̅1̅ or n̅2̅) --- )
           R>         ( (n̅2̅ or n̅1̅)(n1 or n2) --- )
           *          ( n1 XOR n2 --- )
; <Return> OK
1 3 XOR . <Return> 0 OK
0 15 . <Return> 15 OK
```

FORTH also contains bit manipulation words, whose mnemonics can lead to confusion since they are NAD, NOT, OR and XOR.

Respectively, these words carry out their corresponding operations, but in parallel on each bit. Thus

```
1 2 AND . <Return> 0 OK
```

In fact

```
      1  -> 0000 0001
      2  -> 0000 0010
1 AND 2  -> 0000 0000
```

While

```
1 2 + . <Return> 3 OK
```

3.5 STRUCTURE CONTROL WORDS

The user will be particularly interested in these words, because he knows that the quality of the program will depend on their proper use.

In fact, putting them to elegant use will be the culmination of a good analysis of the problem, clear and precise ideas, as well as a comprehensive understanding of what needs to be done.

They allow the user to write a flexible, readable and well-balanced program - all extremely valuable characteristics when one wants to produce programs with a long and useful life.

They include the classic conditional and repeat statements, each word requiring parameters that are taken from the stack as usual.

3.5.1 The Conditional Statement IF ... ELSE ... THEN
The flowchart of such a structure is as shown in figure 3.1.

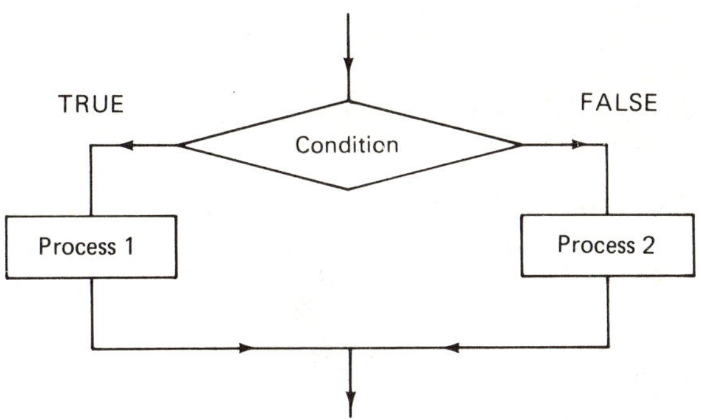

Figure 3.1

We should remember that, in the spirit of FORTH, every parameter used by a word must first be present on the stack. Some readers might be alarmed at this. In fact, the classic syntax 'IF conditions ...' has the following equivalent in FORTH: 'conditions IF ...'.
The corresponding FORTH syntax will be

Condition IF process 1 ELSE process 2 THEN.

Only the boolean value present on the stack at the moment when the IF is executed determines the choice of process

```
b=TRUE   process 1
b=FALSE  process 2
```

The effect of these words on the stack is written

```
IF      ( b --- )
ELSE    ( --- )
THEN    ( --- )
```

Example Say we want to create our word INTERVAL. We can now allow ourselves to make the second test (N Binf) only if the first (N Bsup) is shown to be true

```
: INTERVAL        ( Binf n Bsup --- )
     OVER         ( Binf n Bsup n --- )
     >            ( Binf n b1 --- )
     IF
        <         ( b2 --- )
     ELSE
        2DROP
        0
     THEN
; <Return> OK
```

We can easily use several of these structure by nesting them.

As our example here, we shall illustrate a FORTH word that allows a string of characters to be displayed on the output peripheral. This is the word {."}.

The string of characters must be placed after this word and is terminated with the character {"}.

Example

```
: GOOD-DAY ."  HOW ARE YOU?" ; <Return> OK
GOOD-DAY <Return> HOW ARE YOU? OK
```

We now want our word INTERVAL no longer to return to the boolean variable on the stack, but to display one of the three following responses: too small, good, too big. We write

```
: INTERVAL
       OVER
       >
       IF
          <
          IF
             . "GOOD"
          ELSE
             . "TOO SMALL"
          THEN
       ELSE
          2DROP
          . "TOO BIG"
       THEN
; <Return> OK
```

3.5.2 Repeat Structures

a) The definite loop DO ... LOOP

Figure 3.2 shows the algorithm.

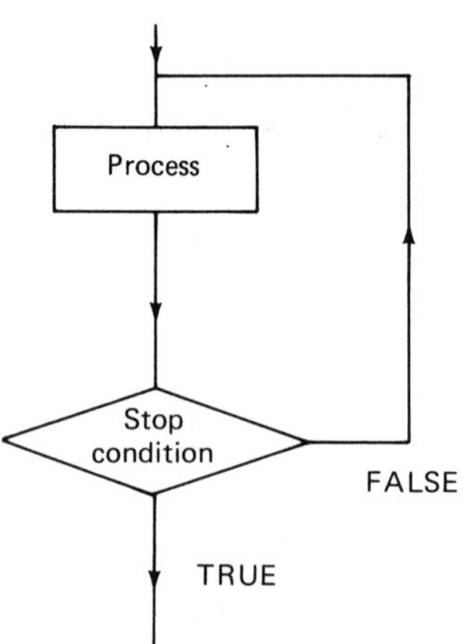

Figure 3.2

The action of the words on the data stack is written

```
DO      ( Ind(End)+1 Ind(Begin) --- )
LOOP    ( --- )
```

These two words carry out the following actions.

DO places the terminating index +1 on the return stack, as well as the starting index; then initiates execution of the words of the process to be repeated.

LOOP compares the two values at the top of the return stack. If the top value is less than the one beneath it, LOOP increments the top value by 1 and transfers execution to the word that immediately follows DO. In the opposite case, the return stack is cleared of its top two values, and execution passes to the first word following LOOP.

We note straight away that the body of the loop will execute at least once.

Example Display all the numbers from 1 to 10.

```
: DISPLAY 1         ( 1 --- )
          10 0      ( 1 10 0 --- )
          DO        ( 1 --- )
             DUP    ( 1 1 --- )
             .      ( 1 --- )
             1+     ( 2 --- )
          LOOP
          DROP      ( --- )
; <Return> OK
DISPLAY <Return> 1 2 3 4 5 6 7 8 9 10 OK
```

We now introduce a practically useful word in the context of this structure: the word I. This word duplicates the top of the return stack on the data stack, this being the current index when executing a DO ... LOOP.

Example DISPLAY can be defined in a different way.

```
: DISPLAY
        11 1   ( 11 1 --- )
        DO     ( --- )
         I .   ( --- )
        LOOP   ( --- )
; <Return> OK
```

Loops can also easily be nested. Suppose we want to display a square of asterisks in three columns and three rows. We write

```
: SQUARE
        CR
        3 0        (number loop rows)
        DO
          3 0      (number loop columns)
          DO
           . "*"
          LOOP
          CR
        LOOP
; <Return> OK
```

The word CR transmits the ASCII code 13 (carriage return) to the output peripheral and causes the display to move to the next line.

```
SQUARE <Return>
***
***
***
OK
```

Just as the word I duplicates the number of the loop being executed, there is a word J which duplicates on the data stack the number of the loop at the level immediately above, that is, the third cell of the return stack.

One can envisage an artificial way of coming out of a loop which consists in replacing the top of the return stack with the contents of the second cell. A word that does this is the word LEAVE. It may be defined as

```
: LEAVE
     R>          ( Save return address for LEAVE )
     R> R>       ( Cell cell2 --- )
     DROP DUP    ( Cell1 cell1 --- )
     >R >R
     >R          ( Restore return address )
; <Return> OK
```

Note though that this word is only used to escape from inextricable situations caused by bad preparation and a bad choice of control structure. Its use is therefore not recommended.

If the programmer wants to increment his current number by a number other than 1, he can use the syntax

```
DO ...+LOOP         +LOOP       ( Incr --- )
```

For this the increment will have to be located on the data stack at the time of execution of the +LOOP. The general functioning of this structure is identical to that of DO ... LOOP.

Example

```
: TABLE         ( n --- )
    DUP         ( n n --- )
    10 * 1+     ( n 10n+1 --- )
    OVER        ( n 10n+1 n --- )
    DO
        I .     ( n --- )
        DUP
    +LOOP
    DROP
; <Return> OK
5 TABLE <Return> 5 10 15 20 25 30 35 40 45 50 OK
```

b) The infinite loop BEGIN ... AGAIN
Figure 3.3 illustrates the algorithm.

Actions on the stack

```
BEGIN  ( --- )
AGAIN  ( --- )
```

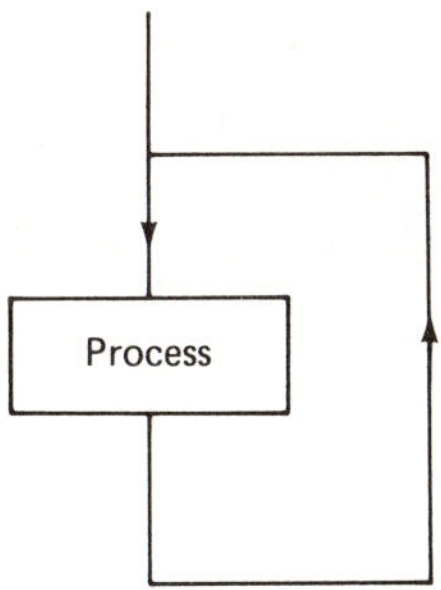

Figure 3.3

This structure is of relatively little interest since there is no means of coming out of it gently. The infinite loop remains the programmer's source of shame.

However, it can be used in process control systems and operating systems. In the FORTH system, for example, it is used for the keyboard interpreter, to which control is returned at the end of execution of all input. We leave it to the reader to devise his own examples.

c) The indefinite loop BEGIN ... UNTIL

Figure 3.4 shows the algorithm.

Actions on the data stack

```
BEGIN   ( --- )
UNTIL   ( b--- )
```

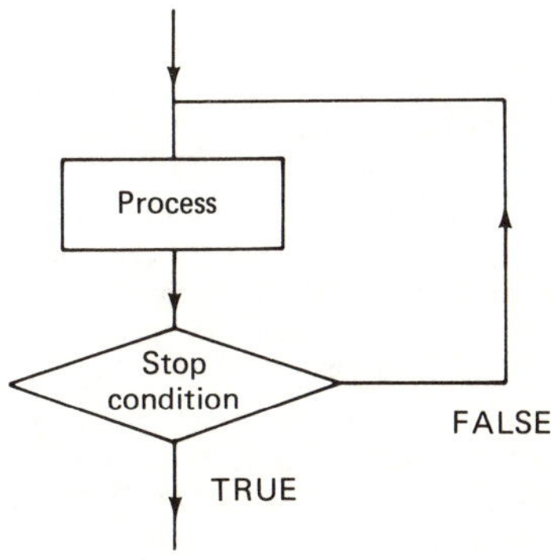

Figure 3.4

Here the branch occurs at the level of UNTIL only if the boolean variable at the top of the stack has a TRUE value. If not, execution is transferred to the following word BEGIN.

Here again it will be noted that the process is carried out at least once.

Suppose for example we have available the two FORTH words OPEN and CLOSE whose respective actions are to turn a tap on and off.

Suppose also that execution of a word {FULL?} returns to the stack a boolean variable having the value TRUE if the wash basin is full.

The word FILL can now be defined as follows

```
: FILL OPEN BEGIN FULL? UNTIL CLOSE ; <Return> OK
```

This structure can very often be used with advantage to replace a bad use of DO ... LOOP, in problems where the introduction of final numbers is purely artificial, and where the exit condition often arises before coincidence of the numbers.

d) The structure BEGIN ... WHILE ... REPEAT

The flowchart is shown in figure 3.5.

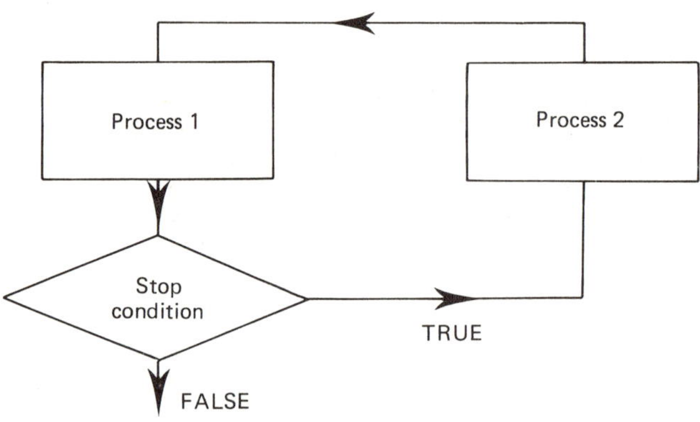

Figure 3.5

Effect of the words of the stack

```
BEGIN    ( --- )
WHILE    ( b--- )
REPEAT   ( --- )
```

This structure is by far the most useful, since it allows the branch point to be placed anywhere in the loop.

In fact, the branch occurs at the level of WHILE.

Branching will occur if the boolean variable then present on the stack takes the value FALSE.

Furthermore, it is important to remember that in the use of this structure it is not sufficient to place 0 on the stack if one wants to come out of the loop, it is also necessary to place a non-null value there if one wants to stay in it! This remark is also valid for BEGIN ... UNTIL, with the exception of the boolean variable.

For our example, let us suppose that we have a word FLOW which turns on a tap for a very short time. We can then define FILL as follows

```
: FILL
      BEGIN
           FULL?  ( b--- )
           0=     ( b--- )
      WHILE
           FLOW
      REPEAT
; <Return> OK
```

All the structures that we have just reviewed can be nested, the only limitation being the machine's memory capacity.

At the end of the book we shall find many instances of their application in problem solving.

3.6 INPUT/OUTPUT

3.6.1 The Keyboard

Like all the high-level languages, FORTH has the facility for interrogating the keyboard. It can do this both at the character and the complete string levels.

The word that works on a character is the word KEY. When executed it causes the interpreter to wait for a keyboard stroke and, when a key is struck, returns the ASCII code of the corresponding character to the stack.

```
KEY   ( ---C )
```

Example We shall define a word that will wait for a key to be struck, display the code of the corresponding character and repeat this operation until the <Return> key is struck. The code for the latter is ASCII 13.

```
: ASCII
      BEGIN
          KEY    ( c--- )
          DUP    ( c c--- )
          13 -   ( c c-13--- )
      WHILE
          .      ( --- )
      REPEAT
      DROP       ( --- )
; <Return> OK
```

Important note The numbers appearing in a definition are converted into binary according to the current base. Here, <Return> has the ASCII code 13 in decimal. If you type this definition in hexadecimal, you will need to replace 13 by OD.

Since the definition is semi-compiled, a subsequent change of base will of course have no effect on the values contained in the definition.

A second word holds up execution until input is received from the keyboard. This is EXPECT. However, this word waits for a complete string of characters whose length and range have been specified by the user.

```
EXPECT   ( Addr u --- )
```

The address corresponds to the first byte in memory from which we want to store the string of characters. The unsigned number corresponds to the maximum length of this string, and the interpreter takes over when this limit is reached, or the <Return> key is struck.

The definition of EXPECT starting from KEY may be written as follows.

```
: EXPECT                      ( addr u --- )
        0                     ( addr u 0 --- )
        BEGIN
            2DUP              ( addr u len u len --- )
            -                 ( addr u len u-len --- )
            IF
              ROT             ( u len addr --- )
              KEY             ( u len addr c --- )
              DUP             ( u len addr c c --- )
              13 -            ( u len addr c c-13 --- )
              IF
                 DUP EMIT
                 OVER         ( u len addr c addr --- )
                 C!
                 1+           ( u len addr+1 --- )
                 ROT ROT      ( addr+1 u len --- )
                 1+           ( addr+1 u len+1 --- )
                 0            ( addr+1 u len+1 0 --- )
              ELSE
                 2DROP DROP   ( ---                  )
                 1            ( 1 ---                )
              THEN
            ELSE
              2DROP 2DROP     ( ---                  )
              1               ( 1 ---                )
            THEN
        UNTIL
; <Return> OK
```

We shall now provide ourselves with a tool that will be very valuable to us later. This is the word DUMP, which will display an area of memory on the screen.

```
DUMP    ( addr n--- )
```

The address corresponds to the beginning of the area of memory to be displayed, and the number n to the number of bytes.

This word can be defined as follows

```
: DUMP
      0       ( addr n num-beg --- )
      DO
        DUP   ( addr addr --- )
        I
        +     ( addr addr+I --- )
        C@    ( addr M --- )
        .     ( addr --- )
     LOOP
     DROP     ( --- )
; <Return> OK
```

We can now make the following test

```
HEX <Return> OK
C000 10 EXPECT <Return> ABCDEFGHIJKLMNOP OK
C000 10 DUMP <Return> 41 42 43 44 45 46 47 ... OK
```

We find displayed the ASCII codes of the characters typed.

Once the line has been taken by the two words already described, it must be put in sequence in order to prepare the work of the interpreter.

The first thing to be done is to isolate the words. The word WORD does this by placing the next following word in the sentence at the end of the dictionary (HERE). The word in memory is preceded by a byte containing its length. The user is free to choose the separator; generally a space is used.

```
WORD   ( c --- )
```

To appreciate fully the action of WORD, we shall define the following word

```
: TEST 32 WORD HERE    ( addr --- )
       6 DUMP          ( --- )
; <Return> OK
TEST ABCD <Return> 4 65 66 67 68 72 OK
```

In some versions of FORTH, WORD returns the address of the beginning of the word in memory, and you will not need to use a variable HERE.

In such a version you would define TEST as follows

```
: TEST 32 WORD 6 DUMP ; <Return> OK
```

The problem with WORD is that it transfers the word to the end of the dictionary; into an area of memory therefore which is extremely variable, since every new definition is placed there. When we remind you also that the interpreter itself uses WORD and this area of memory, you will understand that it is better for our word not to remain there for too long.

To alleviate this problem, FORTH has a buffer area whose address is permanently held in the user variable PAD.

There is therefore a word equivalent to WORD which transfers the next word in the sentence to this buffer zone, instead of to the end of the dictionary. This is the word TEXT.

```
TEXT    ( c--- )
```

Here c corresponds to the ASCII code of the delimiter character. But in this case the string in memory is not preceded by its length. As with the test for WORD, we can make the following test

```
: TESTO
      32 TEXT
      PAD
      6 DUMP
; <Return> OK
TESTO ABCD <Return> 65 66 67 68 32 32 OK
```

Once the word has been transferred into memory by WORD, one often needs to obtain the length of the word as well as the address where it really begins. The address returned by WORD is that of the byte preceding the word and which contains its length.

FORTH has a word to carry out this task, namely

```
COUNT     ( addr --- addr+1 u )
```

It can easily be defined

```
: COUNT          ( addr --- )
     DUP 1+      ( addr addr+1 --- )
     SWAP C@     ( addr+1 u --- )
; <Return> OK
```

For those readers whose basic FORTH does not possess the word TEXT, it can be defined as follows.

```
: TEXT
      PAD
      72 32 FILL
      WORD
      HERE
      COUNT
      PAD SWAP
      <CMOVE
; <Return> OK
```

3.6.2 The Screen: Simple Display Problem

We have already used the basic words {.}, {D.} and {U.}, whose respective roles are to display the value of the top of the stack as single-length, double-length and unsigned numbers. We have also seen {."} which displays a character string terminated by {"}. The word CR causes a carriage return, moving to the beginning of the next line.

We shall now look at the basic tool for all screen manipulation. This is the word EMIT which displays on the screen the character whose ASCII code is on the top of the stack.

We shall first point out the difference between {.} and EMIT.

Example

```
65 <Return> OK
 . <Return> 65 OK
65 <Return> OK
EMIT <Return> A OK
```

The word {CR} is defined from EMIT

```
: CR 13 EMIT ; <Return> OK
```

This type of screen control word is always defined in the same way.

Example Displaying a space character

```
: SPACE 32 EMIT ; <Return> OK
```

In order to display a variable number of spaces, all that is required is to place this number on the stack and use the word SPACES defined as follows.

```
: SPACES 0 DO SPACE LOOP ; <Return> OK
```

As a small diversion, using the control characters available on your keyboard try to create the following words.

PAGE which displays a clear blank screen
BEEP which emits a bleep
SETAB which positions a horizontal tabulation
TAB which positions the cursor at the next horizontal tabulation.

Let us look at a rather more complicated example. How to display on the screen n characters whose ASCII codes are contained in a memory area beginning at a given address ADDR.

```
: TYPE       ( Addr n --- )
  0 DO       ( Addr --- )
  DUP C@     ( Addr c --- )
  EMIT       ( Addr --- )
  1+
  LOOP       ( Addr+1 --- )
  DROP       ( --- )
; <Return> OK
```

Here is another application of the keyboard and the screen.

```
: PLAY CR
  BEGIN
  32 WORD              (Transfers word to end of dictionary)
  HERE 1+ C@           (Value of first character)
       WHILE           (Test for end)
       HERE   COUNT    (Prepares parameters for TYPE)
       TYPE            (Prints word)
       CR
  REPEAT
; <Return> OK
PLAY AT HOME           <Return>
AT
HOME
OK
```

The interpreter detects and executes the words in the input stream in succession. Detection is by means of the separator - here a space. The word that we have just defined examines the remainder in the input stream on execution, carries out the same detection task as the interpreter and displays each separate word found on a new line on the screen. It stops when it reaches a null character.

Another word which will be found to be very useful is -TRAILING which recalculates the length of a string and removes the spaces at the end of a string.

```
-TRAILING     ( Addr u1 --- Addr u2 )
```

Formats
We shall look at the formatting of unsigned double-length numbers; we shall then see what we have to do to apply it to other types of number.

The function of formatting is to construct the character string to be printed which represents the value found at the top of the stack in the current base.

Expression of the print format is enclosed by the words <# and #>. The simplest format consists in converting a (double-length) number at the top of the stack into its literal expression in the form of ASCII codes. This is done by the word #S.

The word {UD.} is defined as follows

```
: UD. <# #S #> TYPE ; <Return> OK
```

You will see that once the format has constructed the required character string, the word #> prepares on the stack the parameters necessary for the word TYPE that carries out the printing.

It should be noted that the word #S will not generate non-significant zeros but always at least one digit.

To format a number more precisely one must be able to convert each of the digits separately. This is done by the word # which places the ASCII code of the least significant digit in the string to be edited and removes it from the number.

Example

```
: DISP2 <# # # #> TYPE ; <Return> OK
  325. DISP2 <Return> 25 OK          ( --- )
```

The possibility of coding digits one by one allows characters to be inserted between digits by means of the word HOLD, preceded by the ASCII code that one wants to insert.

Example
Editing after fixed-point calculation to two decimal places.

```
: .# <# # # 46 HOLD #S #> TYPE ; <Return> OK
123459. .# <Return> 1235.49 OK
```

Remember that the interpreter identifies double-length values by an included decimal point (see previous example).

Do not try to make a comparison between the FORTH concept of format and that of other current high-level languages.

For example, FORTH allows you even to change base within a format. This is because the method of construction of the character string is not hidden.

Example How to display the time, given the number of seconds at the top of the stack.

```
: SEXTAL 6 BASE ! ; <Return> OK
: :00 # SEXTAL # DECIMAL 58 HOLD ; <Return> OK
: SEC <# :00 :00 #S #> TYPE ; <Return> OK
14875. SEC <Return> 4:07:55 OK
```

The word SIGN allows us to work on signed numbers. It tests the sign of the third element in the stack and, if it is negative, inserts the ASCII code for a minus sign in the character string being built up.

The different types of number are prepared for formatting by the following.

Type of number to be formatted	Preparation
32 bits unsigned	---
31 bits unsigned	SWAP OVER DABS
16 bits unsigned	0
16 bits signed	DUP ABS 0

The preparation assumes that SIGN will be used, as described above, on signed numbers, but that it will not be used in the case of unsigned numbers.

3.7 Summary

Word	*Syntax*	*Definition*
@	@(Addr --- Val)	Reads a 16-bit value held at the memory location whose address is at the top of the stack and stores it at the top of the stack
?	?(Addr ---)	Reads a 16-bit value held at the memory location whose address is at the top of the stack and displays it on the screen
HEX	HEX	The current base becomes hexadecimal
DECIMAL	DECIMAL	The current base becomes decimal
!	!(Val Addr ---)	Stores, at the location whose address is at the top of the stack, the 16-bit value that is beneath it. Both elements disappear in the process
C@	C@(Addr --- Val)	Reads an 8-bit value held in the memory location whose address is at the top of the stack and stores it on the stack
C!	C!(Val Addr ---)	Stores, at the location whose address is at the top of the stack, the 8-bit value that is beneath it
CONSTANT	Val CONSTANT Name	Defines a constant called 'Name' and gives it the value 'Val'
VARIABLE	Val VARIABLE Name	Defines a variable called 'Name' and gives it the value 'Val'
DUP	DUP(n --- n n)	Duplicates the item at the top of the stack
DROP	DROP(n ---)	Discards the item at the top of the stack

Word	*Syntax*	*Definition*
SWAP	SWAP(n1 n2 --- n2 n1)	Exchanges the two values at the top of the stack
OVER	OVER(n1 n2 --- n1 n2 n1)	Copies the second item in the stack and places it at the top of the stack
ROT	ROT(n1 n2 n3 --- n2 n3 n1)	Rotates the third item to the top of the stack
2DUP	2DUP(d --- d d)	Duplicates a double-length word on the stack
2DROP	2DROP(d ---)	Discards a double-length word
2SWAP	2SWAP(d1 d2 --- d2 d1)	Exchanges the two double-length words at the top of the stack
2OVER	2OVER(d1 d2 --- d1 d2 d1)	Leaves a copy of the second double-length item in the stack at the top of the stack
2ROT	2ROT(d1 d2 d3 --- d2 d3 d1)	Rotates the third double-length item to the top of the stack
<#		Begins the formatting of numbers. Expects a 32-bit signed number on the stack
#		Each # generates a digit. If there are insufficient, a zero will appear for every #
#S		Free format. Each number is converted to a character
HOLD	HOLD(c ---)	Inserts into the string being formatted a character whose ASCII code is on the stack
SIGN		Inserts a minus sign if the third number in the stack is negative. Usually used immediately before #>
#>		Marks the end of formatting. The string address and character count are left on the stack, ready for TYPE
>R	>R ds:(n ---) rs:(--- n)	Transfers the value at the top of the data stack to the return stack
R>	R> ds:(--- n) rs:(n ---)	Transfers the value at the top of the return stack to the data stack
+	+ (n1 n2 --- n1+n2)	Adds the two items at the top of the stack. The operands disappear and the result is stored at the top of the stack
-	- (n1 n2 --- n1-n2)	Subtracts the two items at the top of the stack

Word	*Syntax*	*Definition*
*	* (n1 n2 --- n1*n2)	Multiplies the two items at the top of the stack. The result is stored there
/	/ (n1 n2 --- Q(n1/n2))	Carries out integer division of the top two items on the stack, replacing them by the result
MOD	MOD (n1 n2 --- R(n1/n2))	Returns the remainder from the integer division of the top two items on the stack
/MOD	/MOD (n1 n2 --- R(n1/n2) Q(n1/n2))	Divides the two items at the top of the stack. Returns the quotient and the remainder
*/	*/ (n1 n2 n3 --- n1*n2/n3)	Multiplies the second item in the stack by the third; the result is then divided by the first item. The intermediate result is a 32-bit number
ABS	ABS (n --- n)	Returns the absolute value at the top of the stack
NEGATE	NEGATE (n --- -n)	Changes the sign of the number at the top of the stack
MIN	MIN (n1 n2 --- min)	Returns the lesser of two parameters held on the stack
MAX	MAX (n1 n2 --- max)	Returns the greater of two parameters held on the stack
1+	1+ (n --- n+1)	Increments the value at the top of the stack by one
1-	1- (n --- n-1)	Decrements the value at the top of the stack by one
2+	2+ (n --- n+2)	Increments the value at the top of the stack by two
2-	2- (n --- n-2)	Decrements the value at the top of the stack by two
2*	2* (n --- 2*n)	Multiplies the top of the stack by two (arithmetic shift one place to the left)
2/	2/ (n --- n/2)	Divides (integer) the top of the stack by two (arithmetic shift one place to the right)
=	= (n1 n2 --- b)	Tests the equality of two single-length (16 bit) parameters. Returns a boolean value to the stack
<	< (n1 n2 --- b)	Compares two single-length (16 bit) parameters. Returns a boolean value to the stack

Word	*Syntax*	*Definition*
>	> (n1 n2 --- b)	Compares two single-length (16 bit) parameters. Returns a boolean value to the stack
0=	0= (n --- b)	Tests a single-length (16 bit) parameter for zero. Returns a boolean value to the stack
0>	0> (n --- b)	Compares a parameter to zero. Returns a boolean value to the stack
0<	0< (n --- b)	Compares a parameter to zero. Returns a true value on the stack if the number is less than zero
AND	AND (n1 n2 --- n1 AND n2)	Logical bit-wise AND of two single-length parameters
OR	OR (n1 n2 --- n1 OR n2)	Logical bit-wise OR of two single-length parameters
NOT	NOT (b --- b)	Reverses a boolean value. Equivalent to 0=
XOR	XOR (n1 n2 --- n1 XOR n2)	Bit-wise exclusive OR of two single-length parameters
D+	D+ (d1 d2 --- d1+d2)	Adds two 32-bit numbers
D-	D- (d1 d2 --- d1-d2)	Subtracts two 32-bit numbers
DNEGATE	DNEGATE (d --- -d)	Changes the sign of a 32-bit number
DABS	DABS (d --- d)	Returns the absolute value of a 32-bit number
DMAX	DMAX (d1 d2 --- DMax)	Returns the maximum of two 32-bit numbers
DMIN	DMIN (d1 d2 --- DMin)	Returns the minimum of two 32-bit numbers
D=	D= (d1 d2 --- b)	Compares two 32-bit numbers. Returns a true flag to the stack if they are equal
DO=	DO= (d1 --- b)	Tests a 32-bit number for zero
D<	D< (d1 d2 --- b)	Compares two 32-bit numbers. Returns true if d1<d2
D.	D. (d ---)	Displays a 32-bit signed number
DU<	DU< (ud1 ud2 --- b)	Compares two unsigned 32-bit numbers
M+	M+ (d n --- d)	Adds a 32-bit number to a 16-bit number. Returns a 32-bit number
M/	M/ (d n --- n)	Divides a 32-bit number by a 16-bit number. The result is a 16-bit number. All values are signed
M*	M* (n1 n2 --- d)	Multiplies two 16-bit numbers and gives a 32-bit number result

Word	*Syntax*	*Definition*
M*/	M*/ (d n u --- d)	Multiplies a 32-bit number by a 16-bit number, then divides the 48-bit result by a 16-bit number. The result is a 32-bit number
S->D	S->D (n --- d)	Converts a 16-bit number to a 32-bit number
U.	U. (u ---)	Displays a single-length unsigned number
U*	U* (u1 u2 --- ud)	Multiplies two unsigned single-length numbers and returns a signed double-length number
U/MOD	U/MOD (ud u1 --- u2 u3)	Divides an unsigned 32-bit number by an unsigned 16-bit number. Returns the quotient u2, and remainder u3, as unsigned single-length numbers
U<	U< (u1 u2 --- b)	Compares two unsigned single-length numbers
IF xxx THEN yyy ELSE zzz	IF (b ---)	If the boolean value at the top of the stack is true on IF, executes xxx; otherwise executes yyy; continues with zzz regardless
DO...LOOP	DO (n1 n2 ---) LOOP (---)	Finite loop structure. The loop will be repeated as long as the index remains less than the end, with automatic incrementation of the index
DO...+LOOP	DO (n1 n2 ---) +LOOP (n ---)	Like DO...LOOP, except that the index is the value currently on the stack when +LOOP is executed
BEGIN...AGAIN	BEGIN (---) AGAIN (---)	Infinite loop
BEGIN...UNTIL	BEGIN (---) UNTIL (b ---)	Infinite loop that will end if the value on the stack on execution of UNTIL is true
BEGIN xxx WHILE yyy REPEAT	BEGIN (---) WHILE (b ---)	Infinite loop. Always executes xxx. If WHILE is true on execution, yyy is also executed. The loop ends if this value is false
KEY	KEY (---c)	Returns the ASCII value of the next available character from the current input device
EXPECT	EXPECT (Addr u ---)	Waits until u characters are available (or for a carriage return), then stores them starting at the given address
WORD	WORD (c ---)	Reads one word from the input stream, using the indicated character as a delimiter. The

Word	*Syntax*	*Definition*
		string is then stored at the HERE address with its length shown at the head
TEXT	TEXT (c ---)	Reads one word from the input stream, using the indicated character as a delimiter. Then sets the PAD to blanks and stores the word in it
DUMP	DUMP (Addr n ---)	Displays the contents of the first n memory cells beginning at address Addr
COUNT	COUNT (Addr --- Addr+1 u)	Prepares the parameters necessary for TYPE. Supplies the string length at the given address
EMIT	EMIT (c ---)	Displays the character whose ASCII code is held at the top of the stack
-TRAILING	-TRAILING (Addr u1 --- Addr u2)	Recalculates the length of a string by eliminating all trailing blanks
TYPE	TYPE (Addr u ---)	Displays u characters on the screen, beginning at the given address. Not to be confused with DUMP

3.8 EXERCISES

3.1 What is the state of the stack after the following sequences?

a) 1 2 3 ROT SWAP OVER ROT DROP
b) 1 2 3 OVER + ROT OVER * SWAP DROP
c) 1 2 3 * OVER ROT DROP /
d) 1 2 3 + SWAP 5 - *
e) 21 43 56 + 120 /MOD SWAP ....
f) 1 2 3 4 2OVER + SWAP - 2DUP

3.2 Assuming that the variables are stacked as shown, write a FORTH word that will enable each of the following expressions to be evaluated.

a) (a b c d ---)
   ((a+c)* b)/(c+d)
b) (a b c d e ---)
   ((c+e)*(a+c))/((b+d)*(a+c)/e)
c) (a b c ---)
   (((a+c)*b)+(c+b))/((a+c)*a)

3.3 a) Write a FORTH word that calculates the minimum of N values held in memory starting from address Addr.

Beginning: (Addr n ---)
END: (--- Min)

b) Write a word that calculates the maximum of these values.

3.4 a) Write the subtraction of two numbers held on the stack without using - .

b) Write, in FORTH, an unsigned version of */MOD and call it U*/MOD.

3.5 a) Write a word that will fill with zeros an area of memory consisting of N cells beginning at address Addr.

(Addr n ---)

b) Write a word that increments the contents of this memory area by 1.

(Addr N ---)

3.6 a) Write a word that calculates the GCD (Greatest Common Divisor) of two single-length integers at the top of the stack.

(N1 N2 --- GCD)

b) Similarly, write a word that calculates the LCM (Lowest Common Multiple).

(N1 N2 --- LCM)

3.7 Define the word DIV that will carry out the real division of two single-length integers to four decimal places.

The syntax used should be of the following form

10 3 DIV <Return> 3.3333 OK

We use the structure DO --- LOOP, multiplying the remainder by 10 at each pass and carrying out the necessary tests to display the decimal point and to exit from the loop (LEAVE).

3.8 Carry out the previous exercise using the structure BEGIN ... UNTIL.

3.9 Repeat exercise 3.7 using the structure BEGIN ... WHILE ... REPEAT.

3.10 Define the word CONV that displays the binary value of the single-length number on the stack. (Do not cheat by using BASE!)

Example

22 CONV <Return> 10110 OK

3.11 Define the word PRIME that displays in decimal all the prime numbers between 0 and 100.

3.12 Define the word ANALYSIS that will display the number of vowels, the number of consonants and the number of blank spaces contained in the string that follows it.

The syntax used will therefore be

ANALYSIS "string of characters" <Return>

4 Basic Vocabularies

4.1 THE EDITOR

4.1.1 Storing the Source Code

You will no doubt have noted that, up until now, it has been impossible for you to modify the definition of a word without having to redefine it completely.

FORTH is a compromise between compiling and interpreting.

Within the range of interpreted languages, like BASIC, one could envisage the possibility of being able to 'call' the text of a word definition, and make modifications to it which would not affect the rest of the program.

Such a requirement is incompatible with an evolving language like FORTH. The chief obstacle is linked with the method of implementation of the dictionary. The variable length definitions accumulate consecutively in memory. Any change in the length of a definition can lead to huge memory manipulations and inextricable pointer changes.

For this reason, the editing tools of words derived from interpreters are not available.

The solution to the problem is to keep the source text of definitions in an area of memory reserved for that purpose. Special procedures will allow such texts to be handled and semi-compiled, so that the dictionary can be updated.

There must of course be a compromise between the access time and the internal memory available in order to send the text between the live user memory and the auxiliary mass store (mainly disks).

To achieve greater flexibility, it is usual to divide the text into pages and allow the machine to control these pages so that access remains completely transparent for the user.

Experts will recognise this as a simplified instance of virtual memory.

The pages of text therefore appear like a book that the user can leaf through without having to concern himself with the physical location of a page when it is called.

4.1.2 Functional Principle

In the majority of FORTH implementations on microcomputers, the number of pages resident in user memory is fixed and the size of a page will correspond to the physical size of the terminal screen.

To maintain transparency, a page overlay algorithm needs to be provided. The numbering of the pages corresponds to the order of physical recording on the disk.

We should note immediately that a powerful machine, through its operating system, will be capable of offering further facilities (for example, call by name).

In order to give a clear description of how a new page is stored in memory, we shall assume that the following FORTH words are recognised (their definitions are too dependent on the individual machine's operating system to be described in detail here).

#MAX	Constant giving the maximum number of pages that can reside in memory at the same time.
#PAGE	Variable giving the number of pages resident in central memory at any given moment.
NEXTPAGE	Variable giving the location of the next page.
FLAG	Word that returns to the stack a flag indicating if the page at the NEXTPAGE address has been altered without being saved.
+PAGE	Word that updates the NEXTPAGE variable after loading.
MEM<-DISK	Word that executes a page load into central memory at the address specified at the top of the stack.
DISK<-MEM	Word that copies on to disk the page specified at the top of the stack.

The algorithm is then easily written as follows

```
: LOADPAGE
     #PAGE @ #MAX @ <
     IF
         1 #PAGE +!
     ELSE
         FLAG
         IF NEXTPAGE @ DISK<-MEM THEN
     THEN
     NEXTPAGE @ MEM<-DISK
     +PAGE
; <Return> OK
```

The heart of the overlay algorithm of course resides in +PAGE. The principal stages in the resolution of this problem are

FIFO allocation - the oldest of the resident pages is replaced.
Statistical allocation - the least frequently used page is replaced.
Hierarchical allocation - the lowest priority page is replaced.

In conclusion we note that operating systems generally use a combination of these different methods; sometimes the algorithm can even evolve in order to optimise response time.

In FORTH there are the following page control commands

LIST (n ---)	Finds a page in central memory, loads it if it is not resident, and displays its text on the screen.
LOAD (n ---)	Finds a page in central memory, loads it if it is not resident, and directs its text to the interpreter.
FLUSH	Copies on to disk all the pages resident in central memory that have been altered.
EMPTY-BUFFERS	Initialises the page memory.

4.1.3 Commands

All the commands described in what follows are grouped together in the EDITOR vocabulary. Before reading further, make sure that this vocabulary is available on your machine.

In their developed form, editors can come to resemble true word processors. Here we shall restrict ourselves to a fairly basic type of editor, as often used in the information technology field.

Our editor's commands will use two special buffers: the Insert Buffer and the Find Buffer.

As usual, shifts of position within a line are done by a position pointer shown on the screen by a special character inserted in front of the indicated character.

Before work can begin on a page, it must be called to the screen by means of the command LIST. The page will then appear on the screen, with all the lines numbered in the margin.

You can if required make the initial page content blank using the command WIPE. This command only affects the LISTed page.

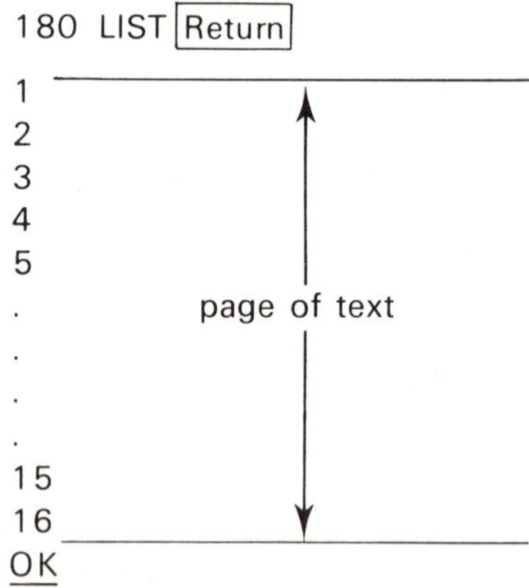

To alter the contents of a line, you must first select the line using the word T (Take).

Example

5 T <Return> 5 OK

This word displays the contents of the chosen line and positions the pointer at the beginning, in front of the first character.

To write on the line the word P (Put) is used

P FRED <Return> OK
5 T <Return>
FRED 5 OK

The word P places the string of characters that follows it in the Input Buffer, then copies the latter into the beginning of the current line (the previous contents of the line disappear).

One method of clearing a line is to type the command P followed by a space

P <Return> OK

Another method of using the word P is to follow it immediately with <Return>. In this way the Input Buffer is not altered and its contents are placed at the beginning of the current line.

This technique can be very useful for copying the contents of the Input Buffer from one line to the next.

```
4 T <Return>
  ↑
P POMPOM <Return> OK
5 T <Return>
  ↑
P <Return> OK
180 LIST <Return>
1
2
3
4 POMPOM
5 POMPOM
.
.
15
16
OK
```

The word F (Find) positions the pointer immediately after the first occurrence of a given string, starting from the current position of the pointer.

```
4 T <Return>
↑POMPOM                                   4 OK
F PO <Return>
PO↑POM                                    4 OK
```

Command I allows a string of characters to be inserted in a line after the current position of the pointer. There is no carry from one line to the next if the insertion causes overflow in a line.

```
I MPO <Return>
POMPO↑POM                                 4 OK
I <Return>
POMPOMPO↑POM                              4 OK
```

Again, it may be seen that commands followed immediately by <Return> work directly on the contents of the buffers without altering them.

Once a string of characters has been located with F, it can be removed by the command E.

```
E <Return>
POMPO↑MPOM                                4 OK
```

These two actions are combined in the command D.

```
D MP <Return>
POMPO↑OM                                  4 OK
```

A more sophisticated command TILL causes the contents of a line to be removed from the current position of the cursor up to and including the first occurrence of a given string.

```
4 T <Return>
↑POMPOM                                          4 OK
P BUT WHERE AND THUS OR NOR FOR <Return> OK
F AND <Return>
BUT WHERE AND↑THUS OR NOR FOR                    4 OK
TILL OR <Return>
BUT WHERE AND↑NOR FOR                            4 OK
```

The command XCH enables strings of characters to be replaced in a line. It places a given string in the Insert Buffer, then transfers it to the current line, replacing the string that is currently pointed to, which is held in the Find Buffer. The operation takes place in two stages: the string contained in the Find Buffer is removed from the line; then the string held in the Insert Buffer is inserted at the current pointer position.

As in the previous examples, the parameter is optional. XCH can work directly on the current contents of the Insert Buffer.

Example

```
5 T <Return>                                     5 OK
 ↑
P THE HUNTER CHASES <Return> OK
F HUNT <Return>
THE HUNT↑ER CHASES                               5 OK
XCH RUNN <Return>
THE RUNN↑ER CHASES                               5 OK
```

The following table summarises the different functions.

Syntax	*Action on buffer*	*Description*
P (ut)	string - IB	Introduction of a line
F (ind)	string - FB	Search for contents of FB in line
I (nsert)	string - IB	Insertion of contents of IB into line
E (rase)		Removal of contents of FB in a line
D (elete)	string - FB	Combination of F and E
XCH	string - IB	Combination of E and I

When text is put on to a blank page, it is satisfying to see the lines increment automatically.

The word P does not produce this, since it assumes that the line has already been selected by means of T. In addition, it has no effect on the pointer in the current line.

The word U makes up for these deficiencies by inserting the string into the currently indicated line, shifting all the subsequent lines downwards; it also increments the line pointer. Lines which are pushed off the screen are lost.

The command X has the opposite function. It removes the current line and shifts those following towards the top of the screen.

The current line is not lost; it is held in the Insert Buffer, ready to be replaced.

As we have already seen, WIPE has a more extreme effect; it clears the entire screen.

The word L, abstracted from LIST, lists the current page, without having to specify its number.

The words N and B are used to move to an adjacent page; they respectively increment and decrement the current page number.

To transfer a line from one screen to another, the word M (Move) can be used; this operates on the current line. It needs two parameters: the number of the destination screen and the line number in that screen. It then makes the insertion. For example, 5 7 M moves the current line to line 7 of screen 5.

The word S searches systematically for a string on consecutive screens starting from the current screen. The parameters required are the number of the last page to be searched and the string to be found. For example,

```
20 S text <Return>
```

searches from the current screen to screen 19 for the string "text".

4.2 THE ASSEMBLER

You will have noticed that, although a high-level language, FORTH contains a certain number of words that allow one to get down to a level very close to the architecture of the machine (for example, manipulation of memory elements, access to input/output ports, etc.).

There are however certain cases where only a real assembler can solve such problems as

1) when you want to speed up the execution of your procedures by optimising the code. Examples are the connection of high throughput peripherals, or the handling of interrupts.
2) when you need to access the internal registers of the processor. A classical example is to execute a different block of code by directly modifying the contents of the program counter.

Accepting the need for access to the assembler, we shall aim to satisfy it, within the framework of the FORTH philosophy.

The standard versions of BASIC have the following answer to the problem. Assuming that we have a written machine code procedure resident in memory and preferably terminating with Ret, a BASIC command allows us to jump to this routine by modifying the contents of the CPU registers, in a manner similar to a Call.

It is most desirable for this routine to be thoroughly tested beforehand since BASIC does not contain any advanced form of editor-assembler to debug it.

The corresponding solution offered by FORTH is much more flexible, since it enables machine code to be generated from FORTH.

What are the tools required for this?

The first requirement is to be able to signal to the interpreter that what follows in the definition of the word is no longer strictly speaking FORTH, but directly executable code.

The second and last requirement is to be able to integrate the stated code into the dictionary, in sequence in the definition.

The first tools required are the two words CODE and ENDCODE. CODE needs to create the header for the word about to be defined, in such a way that any following machine code can be executed. In FIG-FORTH the definition of CODE is simple; it is just a renamed version of create.

```
: CODE CREATE ;
```

It is used as follows to create the header for a machine code definition called WORD

```
CODE WORD
```

The definition of ENDCODE will be given later.

At this point our second tool plays its part. This is in fact the two words {C,} and {,} which transfer the contents of the top of the stack in sequence to the dictionary, respectively on 1 and 2 bytes.

The general structure of a definition containing machine code is therefore

```
CODE WORD xx C, xxxx , (etc.)
```

where xx and xxxx represent object codes expressed in the current base.

It is therefore up to you to see that the program returns to the FORTH interpreter. All you need to do is to terminate your code with a jump to the entry point of the FORTH interpreter.

It is of course quite obvious that in most cases you will have to begin by first saving all the registers before using them and then restore them to their initial values before returning to the interpreter.

Example Let us take the well known case of the Z80 assembler, using the simple problem of clearing the area of memory lying between FA10 and FAB0. (Be sure to check first that this area is not filled.)

The corresponding assembler program is written as follows (for the remainder of this chapter all numbers are written in hexadecimal).

```
LD HL, FA10    21 10 FA
LD DE, FA11    11 11 FA
LD BC, A0      01 A0 00
LD (HL), 0     36 00
LDIR           ED B0
```

Suppose that the interpreter entry point has the address 6000. In order for your procedure to be integrated into FORTH it will have to appear in the following form

```
PUSH BC   C5
PUSH DE   D5
PUSH HL   E5
.
.
body of procedure shown above
.
.
POP HL   E1
POP DE   D1
POP BC   C1
JP 6000  63 00 60
```

```
 0  CONSTANT BC
10  CONSTANT DE
20  CONSTANT HL
```

We can now define the word PUSH as

```
: PUSH C5 + C, ;
```

and use it to replace the three words PUSHBC, PUSHDE AND PUSHHL by the equivalent

```
BC PUSH
DE PUSH
HL PUSH
```

Although we have now used four definitions in place of the original three, the advantages begin to become apparent when we further define POP as

```
: POP  C1 + C, ;
```

so that we can also use

```
BC POP
DE POP
HL POP
```

Furthermore, PUSH and POP are very similar, only differing in the numeric value included in their definitions; it ought to be possible to combine them as two cases of a single, more general, definition.

A good basis in theory, together with a thorough familiarity with FORTH and with your own system should however enable you to solve the problem.

4.3 SUMMARY

LIST	"No. page"LIST	Displays the requested page after perhaps loading from disk if it was not already in memory
LOAD	"No. page"LOAD	Compiles the contents of the requested page, after loading from disk if not held in memory
FLUSH	FLUSH	Clears the block buffers after first saving to disk those that have been modified
EMPTY-BUFFERS	EMPTY-BUFFERS	Empties the block buffers
EDITOR	EDITOR	Makes EDITOR the context vocabulary
T	"No. line"T	Selects the requested line on the work page, displays it and positions the cursor at the beginning of the line
P	- P "string"	Places "string" in the insert buffer which in turn replaces the current line

	- P <Return>	Empties the insert buffer and the current line
	- P <Return>	Replaces the current line with the contents of the insert buffer
I	- I "string"	Inserts the string "string" after the cursor in the current line and in the insert buffer
	- I <Return>	Inserts the contents of the insert buffer in front of the cursor
E	E	Deletes from the current line the first occurrence of the character string contained in the find buffer
D	D "string"	Deletes from the current line the first occurrence of the character string after placing this string in the find buffer
F	- F "string"	Places the character string in the find buffer, locates the first occurrence in the current line and positions the line pointer
	- F <Return>	Locates the first occurrence of the character string held in the find buffer in the current line and positions the line pointer
TILL	TILL "string"	Deletes from the current line all the characters lying between the line pointer and the first occurrence of the character string
XCH	XCH "string"	In the current line exchanges the character string held in the find buffer for the string that follows the command
U	U "string"	Inserts a line under the current line, while observing the functions of P
X	X	Deletes the current line and shifts the remaining lines upward
L	L	Lists the current page on the screen
N	N	Increments the current page number by 1
B	B	Decrements the current page number by 1
M	Page Line M	Inserts the current line of the current page under the specified line of the specified page
ASSEMBLER	ASSEMBLER	Makes the ASSEMBLER vocabulary the context vocabulary
CODE		Used as CODE nnnn <mnemonics> ENDCODE machine code primitive with name nnnn to execute the following machine code

ENDCODE		Terminates a machine code definition. It is sometimes replaced by ;C
,	, (n ---)	Takes the contents of the top of the stack and stores it in the first empty cell in the dictionary, incrementing the dictionary end pointer by 2
C,	C, (n ---)	Takes the 8 least significant bits of the value accessible at the top of the stack, stores them in the first empty byte in the dictionary and increments the dictionary end pointer by 1
SMUDGE	SMUDGE	Reverses the validity bit of the most recently created string header in the dictionary.

5 The Mechanics of the Language

5.1 ANATOMY

5.1.1 Memory Map

In this chapter we propose to look at FORTH from the purely technical point of view. You will find the answers to all the questions that you have the right to ask yourself so far as the functioning and internal structure of the tools that you have already become familiar with are concerned.

We shall first examine how FORTH is located geographically in memory. Figure 5.1 shows at the top the first block, the interpreter, which contains the 'living' part of FORTH. It consists of a very small amount of machine code that is only executable, in which you are working most of the time. It ensures the chaining of all the FORTH words. We shall examine it in more detail later.

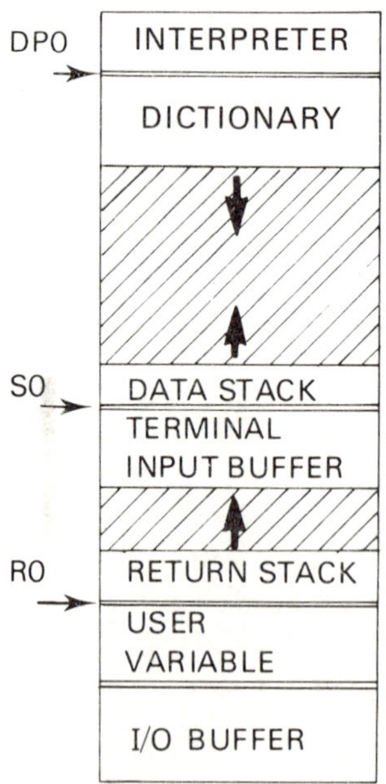

Figure 5.1

The second block is the dictionary. On loading FORTH, it contains the basic FORTH. It extends into the memory as and when new definitions are created.

We have already met the data stack, which follows. It extends in the direction of the dictionary. Access to it is controlled by its stack-like structure. Its base address is in the user variable SO, and its top of stack is accessible by means of the word SP@ which places on the top of the stack the address of the top of the stack (!).

The next part is reserved for your keyboard buffer - the terminal input buffer. This is where FORTH stores all the characters input at the keyboard. It will only show interest in its contents in two instances

a) if the buffer is full

b) if you have hit the return key.

This fixed size buffer is indirectly pointed by S0.

Lower down in memory we find a block of variable size, called the return stack. This is where FORTH stacks the successive return addresses of the procedures.

The base address is held in the user variable R0 and the top of its stack is accessible by means of the word RP@.

The next block contains all the values of the user variables. The words which enable these values to be accessed are of course held in the dictionary.

The last block is reserved for the I/O buffers. It is there that the EDITOR will store the pages that you call.

5.1.2 Dissecting the Dictionary

The dictionary is nothing more than a list of words. Each new word grafted on to the list has a logical link with the one defined immediately before it.

To start off the process, we postulate that the list contains at the beginning a virtual element 'empty'.

Addition of a new word to the dictionary involves the following operations in order

link logically the new word to the last one entered
mark the new word as the last word entered

This is how this mechanism is carried out in practice

the logical link is by means of addresses (Link Field Address)
the 'empty' element has the address 0. (LFA=0)
the LFA address of the last word defined is obtained by using a user variable
although not required by the architecture, the words are stored in a sequential way in order to simplify store management. It is therefore equally necessary to know the first available memory location (DP).

The particular feature of this structure is that it is non-injective; several words in the list can point to the same address and thus have the same antecedent.

This makes it possible therefore to branch the dictionary logically into vocabularies by means of a single set of pointers (see 2.3 and 2.4).

As an exercise, we shall write a FORTH word that counts the number of definitions actually present in the current vocabulary.

```
: COUNT
        0 CONTEXT @
        BEGIN
              @ PFA 4 - DUP
        WHILE
             SWAP 1+ SWAP
        REPEAT
        DROP
; <Return> OK
```

In chapter 2 we introduced the word FORGET, which deletes from the dictionary all the words including and after a given word.

We can now understand its mechanism better. It places in DP the address of the word that precedes the given word in the dictionary.

This lopping of the dictionary is drastic. Every dictionary search begins with the word pointed by DP. All the words defined subsequently are lost.

Nevertheless, FORGET is protected thanks to the user variable FENCE which provides a limit address before which deletions are ignored.

On initialisation, FENCE contains the address of the last word of the basic FORTH.

Thus, for example, at any time you can protect all your work from untimely loss by the following

```
DP @ FENCE ! <Return> OK
```

5.1.3 Observation of a Word in the Dictionary

Let us now look at the structure of a word in the dictionary. Every word contains two parts: a header which enables it to be identified, and a body which defines it.

a) Header

The first byte contains two pieces of information: the length of the word name in the five least significant bits, and the state of the word in two bits (see figure 5.2).

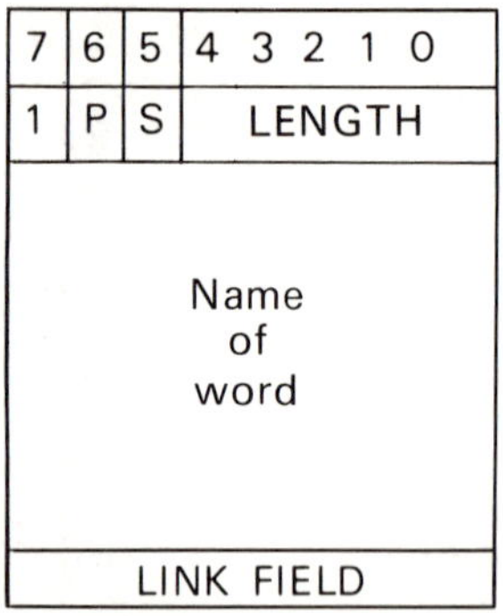

7	6	5	4 3 2 1 0
1	P	S	LENGTH
Name of word			
LINK FIELD			

Figure 5.2

We saw how the Smudge Bit (S) is used in section 4.2. It is set at 1 when the definition of the word is valid.

As for the Precedence Bit (P), it is linked with the concept of the immediate word which will be explained in chapter 6.

Then come the ASCII characters of the word name (0 to 31 characters). The MSB of the last byte is set to 1 to indicate the end of the string.

The convention is that the address of the first byte of the header is called NFA (Name Field Address).

Then there is the zone that ensures chaining in the dictionary. It contains the NFA of the preceding word in the dictionary. This is the LFA (Link Field Address).

The contents of the LFA of the first word in the dictionary is of course null.

b) The body

The begin address of this block is called CFA (Code Field Address). This is where all the data relating to the function of the word start.

This code field can contain three kinds of information

executable code (a word containing ASSEMBLER)
parameters (variables)

or, most usually, a list of the CFAs of the words that go to make it up.

An additional artificial address, called the PFA (Parameter Field Address), is provided because FORTH interposes between the header and the parameters of the word a two-byte piece of information, the use of which we shall explain below. There is therefore always a difference of two between the PFA and the CFA.

There are a certain number of words that allow access to these different addresses. All of them are built around the word {'} (called tick), which places the PFA of a given word on the stack.

Example

```
HEX <Return> OK
' SWAP . <Return> 054B OK
```

We can then easily construct CFA, LFA and NFA in the following way

```
: CFA 2  - ; <Return> OK ( PFA---CFA )
: LFA 2  - ; <Return> OK ( CFA---LFA )
: NFA
      4 -
      BEGIN
           DUP
           80  AND  0=
      WHILE
           1  -
      REPEAT
; <Return> OK
```

NFA examines the bytes of memory in turn, in the direction of decreasing address, until it finds the first whose MSB is set to 1.

Let us look in more detail at the contents of the CFA of any word. The contents of this address point towards machine code within a stated defining word, which in turn depends on the nature of the chosen word.

If the word in question is a variable, execution of the machine code of the corresponding definition word (VARIABLE), whose address is therefore found in the CFA, will place the PFA on the stack, that is, in the address where the value of the variable will be found.

If the word in question is a constant, execution of the code in the corresponding definition word (CONSTANT) will this time place on the stack the contents of the memory element of address PFA, that is, the value of the constant.

If the word in question is a colon definition, execution of the code of the definition word (:) causes execution of the words that make up the definition.

How are these words represented within the definition? Quite simply, by their respective CFAs.

Example

10 VARIABLE WEIGHT <Return> OK

The word WEIGHT will therefore have the structure in the dictionary as shown in figure 5.3.

NFA		86
	W	E
	I	G
	H	T + 80
LFA	NFA of the preceding word	
CFA	Address of the code for VARIABLE	
PFA	Variable value	

Figure 5.3

NFA		84
	M	E
	A	L + 80
LFA	NFA of the preceding word	
CFA	Machine code for :	
PFA	CFA of STARTER	
	CFA of MAIN COURSE	
	CFA of DESSERT	
	CFA of ;	

Figure 5.4

The structure of a constant will be exactly similar, the only difference being the definition word that is pointed to.

Let us now look at the case of a standard colon definition

: MEAL STARTER MAIN-COURSE DESSERT ; <Return> OK

The word MEAL will have the structure shown in figure 5.4.

Given that we now know the structure of the word in the dictionary, we can turn our attention to examining how the interpreter works.

5.1.4 Internal Functioning of the Interpreter
The interpreter is fed word by word, as an input stream. It can handle the words presented to it in one of two ways - compiling or executing them. This choice is determined by the state of a user variable - STATE.

Compilation
Every definition must begin with the word {:}. It is this word that puts the interpreter into compile mode by means of STATE, after establishing the string header in the dictionary. All the words that follow in the input stream are compiled. Their CFA is systematically added at the current position of the dictionary pointer.

You also know that {;} is used to mark the end of every definition. It is this word that puts the interpreter in execution mode.

At this point, the reader may wish to ask the following. If, after meeting the word {:}, the interpreter systematically compiles all the words that follow in the input stream, and if the word {;} is a FORTH word just like any other, how can it have any effect on the state of the interpreter?

In fact, the word {;} belongs to that special category of words which can have a different function depending on the state of the interpreter when it encounters them. We shall learn more about these in chapter 6.

The compiling function of the interpreter therefore consists in adding to the end of the dictionary the CFA of the current word in the input stream. This simple function is carried out by the word COMPILE.

Note that here the concept of input stream is broad; the words can be entered from the keyboard, from pages of the editor (on LOADing), or from any type of interface.

The first task is to recognise the word in the dictionary, in order to obtain its CFA. This function is similar to that of the word {,}.

There are two possibilities

the word exists - then there is no problem
the word does not exist - then the interpreter looks to see if its expression is compatible with a number in the current base. Before placing it in the dictionary, the interpreter interposes the CFA of the special word LITERAL which, on execution, places the following number on the stack. The use of LITERAL avoids any confusion between the number and a CFA to be executed.

Having explained the mechanism by which a definition is constructed from words present in the dictionary, we shall now see how these words are executed.

Execution
What happens when you type a FORTH word at the keyboard of your terminal and start its execution by pressing the <Return> key?

The interpreter, now in execution mode, will place the CFA of this word at the top of the stack and delegate the work to the word EXECUTE.

To illustrate how it operates more clearly, we shall return to a more theoretical example, in this case the problem of a tree structure.

Consider a meal consisting of a starter, a main course, and a dessert. The main course itself consists of chicken and chips. There are two pieces of chicken, the leg and the wing.

It is normal to show the meal as in figure 5.5.

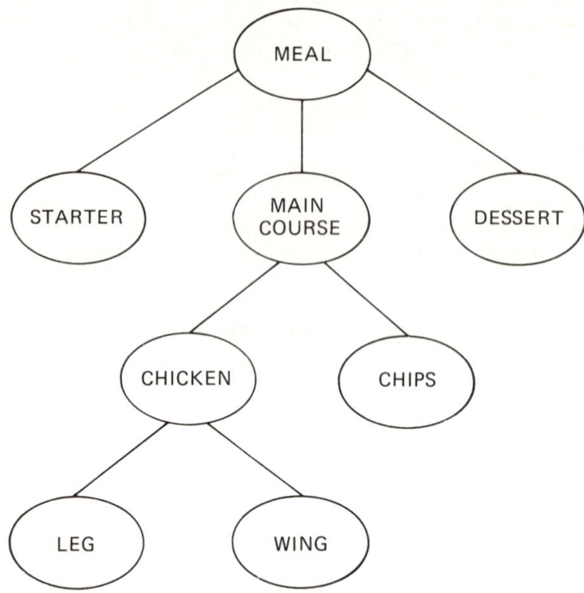

Figure 5.5

The problem is to construct a mechanism that will list all the constituents of the meal in the order in which they will be eaten - that is, starter, leg, wing, chips, dessert.

We need to go through the tree in a coherent way, choosing only the 'leaves'.

As shown in figure 5.5, the tree is not very practical to use, because there is no order relation between nodes of the same level.

Figure 5.6 shows a much more appropriate representation.

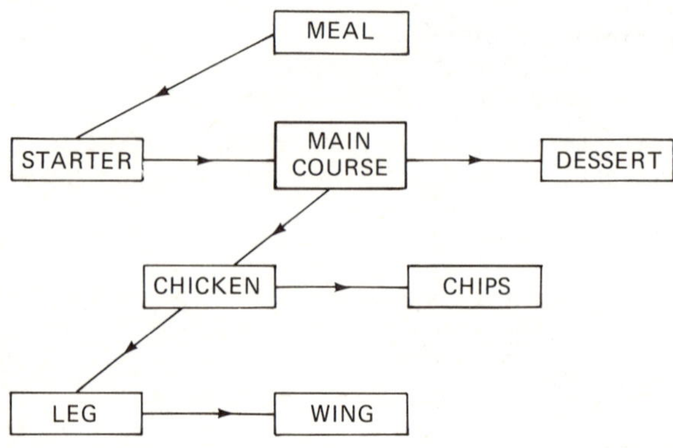

Figure 5.6

It is also necessary to know where to begin, that is, to know the top of the tree. Figure 5.7 presents the problem in diagrammatic form best suited for a data processing system to handle.

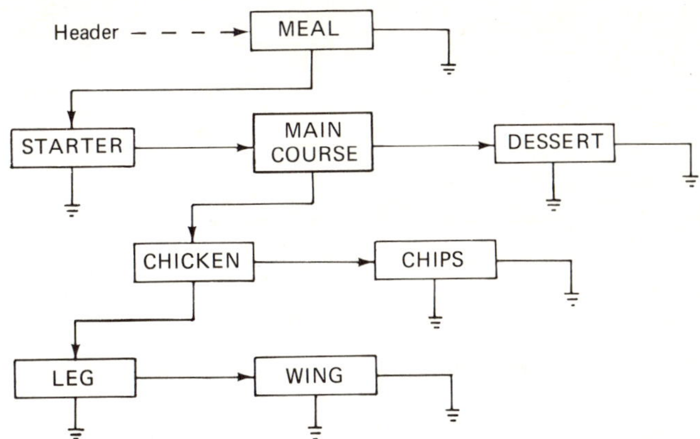

Figure 5.7

We can see that access to one of these boxes will provide the following information

the contents of the box
the address of the 'daughter' box (below)
the address of the 'sister' box (to the right)

These two addresses by convention have the value 0 (empty) when this 'daughter' or this 'sister' do not exist.

The mechanism for walking through this tree is as follows

```
STACK head
REPEAT

    WHILE address ≠ 0 DO
        IF address (daughter) =0 THEN
              EAT contents
              address = address (sister)
        ELSE
              STACK address (sister)
              address = address (daughter)
        END IF
    END WHILE
UNTIL stack = empty
```

The direction of the walk is then as shown in figure 5.8.

The dishes eaten are indicated by bold type boxes.

What can we learn from this example? First, every tree structure exploration requires an auxiliary stack because, after walking a given branch, we need to be able to return to the main trunk in order to explore a new branch. These junction points are used in the reverse order of their being encountered, which corresponds perfectly with the structure of the LIFO stack.

Second, we need markers to indicate the end of branches in order to trigger the unstacking of the preceding junction.

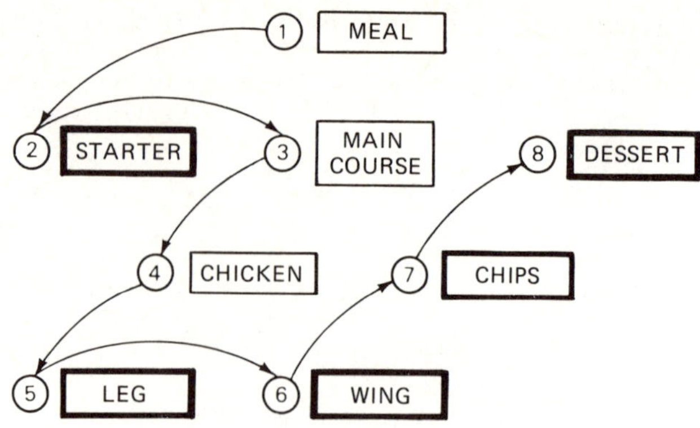

Figure 5.8

You will certainly guess that there was a direct link between this problem and execution of the following FORTH word.

```
: MEAL STARTER MAIN-COURSE DESSERT ; <Return> OK
```

With

```
: MAIN-COURSE CHICKEN CHIPS ; <Return> OK
: CHICKEN LEG WING ; <Return> OK
```

We can isolate three different functions in the algorithm

the tests: the definitions are terminated (flagged) with the word {;} which terminates the horizontal levels. There is no reason to test if there is a lower level because the 'leaves' are composed of assembler, which itself resets the logic for the walk.

control of the stack: stacking is ensured by the word {:}, while {;} ensures removal from the stack. These two words belong to a rather special category of high-level words, to which we shall return in the following chapter.

control of the addresses: this very simple function is carried out by an assembler module consisting of several lines, which is the only part of FORTH that is not integrated into the structure of the dictionary.

The important feature of the FORTH language is that the dictionary is self-sufficient since each word contains the linking logic for execution. This is one of the common functioning principles of the so-called threaded languages.

To convince you of this, let us follow step by step the flow of the word MEAL, immediately after execution of STARTER.

The registers that the FORTH interpreter needs in execution mode are

RP Return Pointer

IP Interpreter Pointer. During execution of a definition, it points permanently to the memory cell containing the CFA of the next word to be executed.

How does the execution of MAIN-COURSE occur?

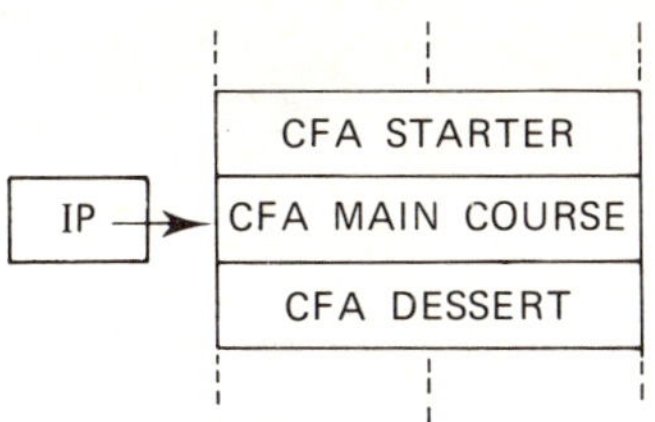

Figure 5.9

IP points to the CFA of main course. Before executing this word, IP is incremented by 2 to make it point to the element containing the CFA of DESSERT. In fact, it points to the word that we shall have to execute when we have finished our main course.

To consume our main course, we need to release the code pointed to by the CFA of the main course.

The first word encountered will save IP in the return stack and place in IP the PFA of MAIN-COURSE. IP thus now points to an element containing the CFA of CHICKEN (see figure 5.10).

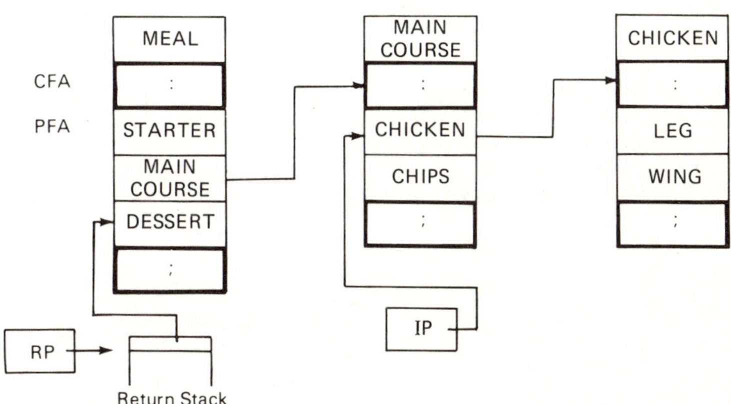

Figure 5.10

As we did before executing MAIN-COURSE, we shall increment IP so that it points to CHIPS on our return from CHICKEN.

The first word met in the consumption of CHICKEN saves IP on the return stack and replaces it with the PFA of CHICKEN, the element containing the CFA of LEG.

Figure 5.11 shows the links.

Let us now move forward to the point where we have finished with the LEG and the WING. We are now going to execute the {;} of CHICKEN, placed in the dictionary after definition at the time of the compiling of CHICKEN.

As usual, before executing the word {;}, the interpreter increments IP, which might cause concern since the definition stops there.

However, execution of {;} puts everything in order, since it replaces the current value of IP with the top of the return stack, which it unstacks.

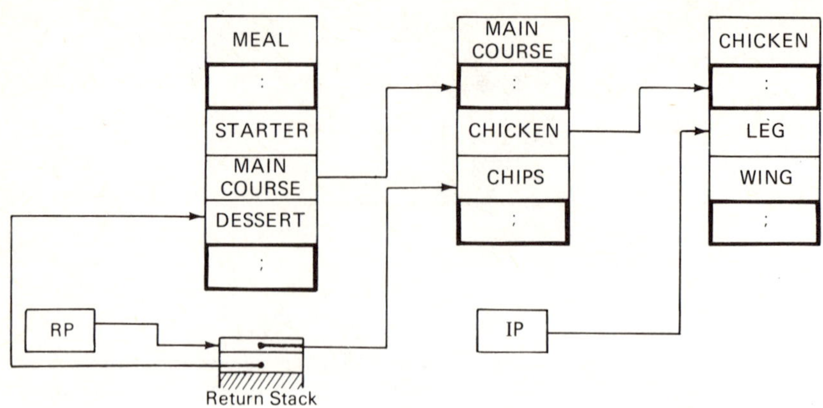

Figure 5.11

IP now points to the CFA of CHIPS, which is the continuation of our menu.

Similarly, execution of the {;} of MAIN-COURSE will replace IP with the contents of the top of the stack, which is of course the CFA of DESSERT.

5.1.5 Initialisation Process

There are three types of initialisation: the data and return stacks, the I/O buffers, and the user variables.

Three words carry out these initialisations: their actions are summarised in the following table.

	Data & Return Stack	*I/O Buffers*	*User Variables*
COLD	Yes	Yes	Yes
WARM	Yes	Yes	No
ABORT	Yes	No	No

The stacks

Stack initialisation is done by putting the value of the user variables S0 and R0 in the stack pointers SP and RP.

The words that carry out these functions are SP! and RP!.

This gives, quite simply

```
: ABORT SP! RP! QUIT ; <Return> OK
```

Note that the effect of ABORT depends on the contents of the user variables R0 and S0 at the moment when it is executed.

QUIT enables one to enter FORTH; section 5.1.6 will give more details of this.

The I/O buffers

The word EMPTY-BUFFERS takes over all initialisation of the user variables that point to these buffers.

```
: WARM EMPTY-BUFFERS ABORT ; <Return> OK
```

The user variables

Rather than initialise them separately, it is simpler to keep a copy of the initial values in a part of memory, so that they can be copied again into the work space.

The definition of COLD will therefore be

```
: COLD
      Address of zone start
      Address of zone end
      Number of bytes
      CMOVE
      WARM
; <Return> OK
```

5.1.6 The FORTH Monitor

In the foregoing presentation of the flow in FORTH, there is one last element that is lacking and which establishes the link between you and the interpreter. This is the QUIT function.

As with any system, you are permanently in a loop, waiting for commands.

The functions of QUIT may be broken down in the following way

- Initialisation of the Return Stack (RP!)
- Waiting for a signal to process (<Return>)
- Interpreting
- Display of OK

The word QUIT can of course also be included in a definition: it puts you back in the initial state. This is why the first word of QUIT carries out the initialisation of the return stack.

Figure 5.12 summarises the general FORTH flowchart.

5.2 IMPLEMENTATION ON DIFFERENT MACHINES

FORTH needs three pointers in order to function

RP Return stack Pointer
SP data Stack Pointer
IP Interpreter Pointer

Generally, microprocessors can control a pointed stack automatically by means of a special register in the CPU, which is accessible to the user.

This stack is used by the CPU to save the values of the program counter when subroutine calls occur. There are also access instructions, such as PUSH and POP which carry out memory access and updating of the stack pointer in a single basic instruction.

The facilities of this automatic control are often used for the data stack.

If a second automatic stack is not available to you, you will have to control the return stack manually.

Two conditions can occur: you may have available enough free registers capable of containing addresses, in which case you can dedicate one to the control of the return stack. If not, you store this pointer in memory at a fixed address.

For IP, the problem is similar. Either allocate it an address register in the CPU, or install it in memory.

If the number of available registers in the CPU is limited (as in the Z80, for example), to set up the three pointers you will have to compromise between the memory and the internal registers.

It will be appreciated that this choice will depend essentially on the machine's facilities.

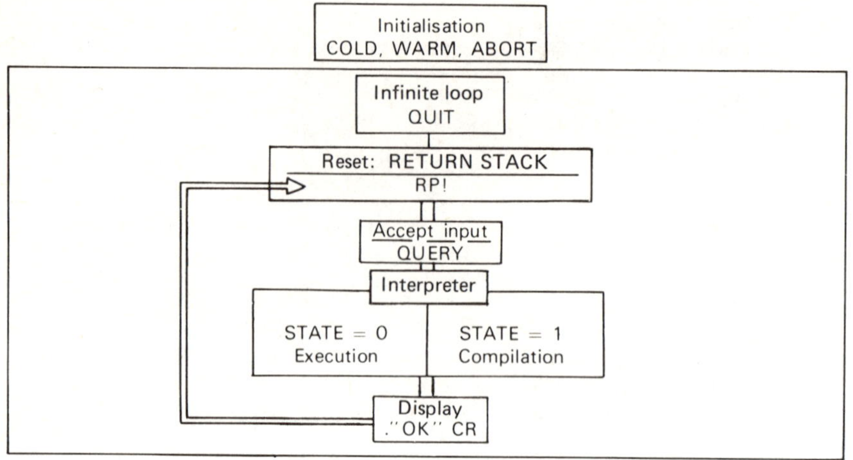

Figure 5.12

To convince you of this, here are two real examples.

The well known Intel 8080 8-bit microprocessor contains the following registers: A,F,B,C,D,E,H,L,PC,SP.

SP is the stack pointer controlled automatically by the machine when instructions of the type PUSH, POP, CALL occur.

PC is the program counter.

(B,C), (D,E), (H,L) are three pairs of registers that are accessible, either individually, or two at a time, to manipulate the addresses.

A is the accumulator and F is the state register of the accumulator.

One of the peculiarities of this microprocessor is that only HL can address the memory; indeed, by convention M = (HL).

SP is naturally taken to control the data stack.

Three machine registers (BC, DE, HL) remain for the two FORTH registers RP and IP.

Programming FORTH words in assembly will be quite intractable if two out of three double registers must remain intact.

The wise programmer therefore for example assigns BC to IP and keeps RP in store.

The choice between RP and IP is immaterial since their functions are closely linked and their requests are equal.

On other machines, the design of the internal architecture is such that internal registers do not have priority over memory, thanks to very sophisticated addressing modes (for example, LSI11 and HP3000).

There is no difficulty in setting all the pointers in memory, and their control remains simple. The parameters to be taken into consideration when allocating are execution time, ease of programming and respect for the restrictions of the operating system.

The second step is to dimension the different blocks that make up FORTH in memory.

The I/O buffers - their size is determined by the number of pages simultaneously resident in memory.

The return stack - of course, its size limits the maximum admissible number of interleavings in a definition.

Terminal Input Buffer - it is desirable to make this the same length as a line on your terminal.

Data Stack - it shares the remainder of the memory with the dictionary.

Once these parameters have been defined, it only remains for you to write the source in assembler, including 10 per cent in executable machine code, the remainder being no more than references to already defined labels.

In other words, the transfer of basic FORTH from one machine to another only requires the translation of this 10 per cent of purely executable code.

5.3 SUMMARY

Word	*Syntax*	*Definition*
PFA	PFA (CFA --- PFA)	Calculates the PFA from the CFA
LFA	LFA (CFA --- LFA)	Calculates the LFA from the CFA
NFA	NFA (CFA --- NFA)	Calculates the NFA from the CFA
CFA	CFA (PFA --- CFA)	Calculates the CFA from the PFA
EXECUTE	EXECUTE (CFA ---)	Executes the word whose CFA is on the stack
COLD	COLD	Initialisation of the stacks, I/O buffer and user variables
WARM	WARM	Initialisation of the stacks and I/O buffers
ABORT	ABORT	Initialisation of the stacks
SP!	SP!	Places the value of the user variable S0 in the stack pointer
SP@	SP@	Places the stack pointer value on the stack
RP!	RP!	Places the value of the user variable R0 in the return stack pointer
RP@	RP@	Places the value of the return stack pointer on the stack
QUIT	QUIT	Initialises the return stack, stops compilation or execution and returns control to the user.

6 High-level Words

6.1 WORDS RELATING TO COMPILATION

6.1.1 Concept of the Immediate and Non-immediate Word

In the preceding chapter we showed how it is possible for certain words to behave differently depending on whether the interpreter is in compiling mode or in execution mode.

The advantage of this facility is to be able to carry out an action during the construction of a definition.

To explain this concept more fully, let us first look at the class of words whose action only takes place at the moment that they are compiled. These are immediate words.

These words are generated very easily; use of the word IMMEDIATE makes immediate the last word that was entered in the dictionary.

Here is an example

```
: CUCKOO ." CUCKOO" ; <Return> OK
IMMEDIATE <Return> OK
: TEST CUCKOO ." COCK-A-DOODLE-DOO" ; <Return> CUCKOO OK
TEST <Return> COCK-A-DOODLE-DOO OK
CUCKOO <Return> CUCKOO OK
```

We can see from this example that, after making our word immediate, if it is subsequently present in a definition, it will be executed on compiling without being considered in that definition.

Furthermore, the property of a word's being immediate does not in any way affect its behaviour when it is directly executed.

The advantage of being able to act at the time of compiling is of course not limited to displaying nonsense on your screen.

Let us try to visualise how the control structures of FORTH are embedded. At the beginning the FORTH words BRANCH and OBRANCH are available. These are very rudimentary GOTOs; they execute relative addressing corresponding to their position in the definition.

```
: -4 -4 ; IMMEDIATE <Return> OK
: EVERYWHERE ." EVERYWHERE" CR ; <Return> OK
: ZOU EVERYWHERE BRANCH -4 ; <Return> OK
```

OBRANCH will make a relative jump on condition that the value at the top of the stack is null.

We shall not devote more space to an examination of words of this type, since they are not to be encouraged in your definitions.

Let us take the very simple case of BEGIN ... AGAIN. On execution, it is in fact sufficient for AGAIN to execute a BRANCH to the label BEGIN. You will see that BEGIN has nothing to execute; at the time of compiling it serves as a marker for the compiling of AGAIN. Its role is certainly immediate, since it prepares the ground for the compiling of AGAIN, but it will no longer appear in the compiled definition.

As always, the transfer of the parameter is carried out by means of the stack, and BEGIN simply stacks the address of the first empty element in the dictionary.

```
: BEGIN HERE ; IMMEDIATE <Return> OK
```

For its part, AGAIN stores the CFA of BRANCH in the first empty element then the relative address of the jump, that is, the difference between HERE and the address placed at the top of the stack by BEGIN.

AGAIN is therefore defined as follows

```
: AGAIN COMPILE BRANCH (places the CFA of BRANCH in the order of
                        the dictionary)
  HERE - ,             (places the relative address of the jump)
  ;
  IMMEDIATE <Return> OK
```

Let us look at the definition of a word using this control structure

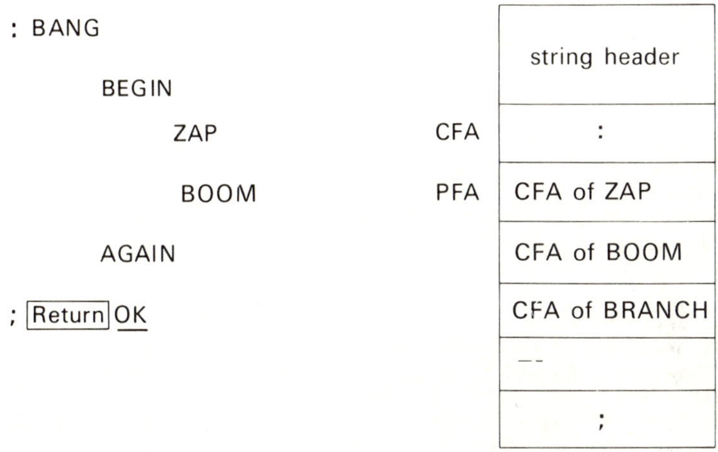

```
: BANG
      BEGIN
            ZAP
             BOOM
      AGAIN
; [Return] OK
```

	string header
CFA	:
PFA	CFA of ZAP
	CFA of BOOM
	CFA of BRANCH
	--
	;

How does the interpreter recognise an immediate word? It is the precedence bit that indicates the immediate character of a word. The function of the word IMMEDIATE is to set the precedence bit of the last word created in the dictionary.

Given that when the interpreter is in compiling mode and meets an immediate word, it executes it, it is good to ask oneself why the interpreter remains in this same mode for the remainder of the definition. In fact, the interpreter always remains in compiling mode when it compiles a definition, even during execution of an immediate word.

When the interpreter finds an immediate word in a definition, it carries out an EXECUTE of this word, which requires no change of mode.

6.1.2 The Word [COMPILE]

Suppose you have defined a word and have made it immediate. It is possible that you may then want to use it in a definition in its normal form, that is, non-immediate. All that is required to solve this problem is to place the word [COMPILE] in front of this word in the definition. This word [COMPILE] tells the interpreter that it should ignore the precedence bit of the word that follows.

Example 1

In some versions of FORTH, the word {'} (tick) is immediate. If you need to work on the PFA of a given word in the execution of a definition, it is necessary to place [COMPILE] in front of {'}.

Suppose we want to obtain the CFA of a word using the syntax {:} CFA word.

If we use {'} in its immediate form without [COMPILE], that is

```
: CFA ' 2- ; <Return> OK
```

The fact of typing in CFA WORD would have the effect of putting the CFA of 2- on the stack and then executing WORD, which is not the aim.

The answer is to inhibit the action of {'} when compiling at the time of execution, giving the following definition of CFA

```
: CFA [COMPILE] ' 2- ;      ( --- CFA )
<Return> OK
```

Example 2

Another application is to create a pseudo-vocabulary of immediate words, that is, to be able to define immediate words from other immediate words.

```
: BOOM ." BOOM" ; IMMEDIATE <Return> OK
: BADABOOM ." BADA" [COMPILE] BOOM ; IMMEDIATE
<Return> OK
```

6.1.3 The Structure [---]

We now turn our attention to the structure that will allow us to make immediate one or a series of words within a definition, but only temporarily.

The word {[} indicates the beginning of the words to be considered immediate, while {]} indicates return to normal compiling.

The one or more words placed within [] retain their same non-immediate character for all future use.

Example

```
: ZONK ." ZONK" ; <Return> OK
: POW [ZONK] ZONK ; <Return> ZONK OK
POW <Return> ZONK OK
: ZAP ZONK ; <Return> OK
```

In the same way that [COMPILE] makes non-immediate the immediate word that follows it in a definition, without however affecting its nature, so the words {[} and {]} have not made ZONK immediate. It is for the user to determine in which form a word will be most frequently used before making a word immediate, so as to avoid weighing down future definitions unnecessarily.

6.1.4 Compile Time and Run Time

We have seen that there are two modes for the interpreter: compiling mode and execution mode.

We know how to define two exclusive types of words: non-immediate words, whose action is carried out when the interpreter is in execution mode, and immediate words, which are executed even when the interpreter is in compiling mode.

The control structures do not however belong to this category, because the majority of the words that go to make them up require two different actions, one on compiling (a compile-time action) and another on execution (a run-time action). This is the case with AGAIN, where

on compiling, it calculates and stores the relative address of BEGIN whose absolute address is at the top of the stack.
on execution, it makes the jump to the address of BEGIN.

We shall now try to establish a method for the solution of this type of problem.

Obviously, the word must act on compiling; it must therefore be immediate. Thus, all the words that make it up will be executed on compiling. There should remain no trace of it in the word being defined, except if execution of the immediate word forces into the definition one or more words to carry out a run-time function.

There are three words (already defined) that allow objects to be forced in the dictionary; these are COMPILE, {C,} and {,}.

COMPILE places the CFA of the word that follows it at the address contained in HERE, that is, at the end of the dictionary.

{C,} and {,} respectively place the top of the stack at the same place (HERE), occupying respectively one or two bytes.

We remind you of the definition of AGAIN with a simple example. Knowing that BEGIN has placed its absolute address on the stack

```
: AGAIN
      COMPILE BRANCH (Forces the CFA of BRANCH)
      HERE - ,       (Calculates the relative address)
; IMMEDIATE <Return> OK
```

Example 1

```
: SPLASH ." SPLASH" ; <Return> OK
: PLOP ." PLOP" ; <Return> OK
: NOISE COMPILE PLOP SPLASH ; IMMEDIATE <Return> OK
: SOUND NOISE ; <Return> SPLASH OK
SOUND <Return> PLOP OK
```

Example 2

We shall try to define the FORTH words of the control structure DO...LOOP.

We analyse the functions of the two words of the structure.

DO Compiling: it stacks its address in the definition.
Execution: it transfers the loop indices to the return stack.

LOOP Compiling: it calculates the relative address of DO.
Execution: it increments the loop index, carries out the test and finally the jump.

```
: DO
    COMPILE SWAP  (Transfers the loop indices to the return stack)
    COMPILE >R
    COMPILE >R
    HERE          (Stacks the absolute address)
; IMMEDIATE <Return> OK
```

```
: LOOP
     COMPILE R>    (Increments the current loop index)
     COMPILE 1+
     COMPILE R>    (Stacks the end address)
     COMPILE 2DUP  (Tests for end of loop and saves
     COMPILE >R     two loop indices)
     COMPILE >R
     COMPILE <
     COMPILE 0=
     COMPILE       (Conditional jump)
     OBRANCH
     HERE - ,      (Forces the jump address)
     COMPILE R>    (Clears the return stack)
     COMPILE R>
     COMPILE 2DROP
; IMMEDIATE <Return> OK
```

As an exercise, define +LOOP and the structure BEGIN...WHILE... REPEAT.

We hope that you are conscious of the power of the tools that FORTH offers through the possibility of creating control structures. If you already know a high-level language, you will appreciate FORTH all the more.

6.2 WORDS RELATING TO THE DEFINITION OF OTHER WORDS

6.2.1 The Definition Validation Bit (Smudge bit)

On several occasions already, we have referred to two specialised bits in the first byte of definitions contained in the dictionary.

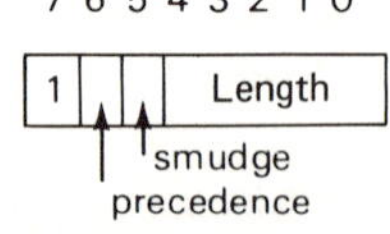

Now that you have a clear idea of how the interpreter functions internally, we shall begin to take a closer look at how these different bits function.

Bit 7 always has the value 1. Why?

You will have noted that you can only access a definition in the dictionary by its LFA. The NFA cannot be immediately calculated in a manner similar to the LFA, since the definition names are of variable length.

Thanks to this bit being systematically forced to 1 at the head of a definition, we are always able to find it quite easily. We only have to search the decreasing addresses for the first byte whose MSB is at 1.

```
: NFA 4 -             ( CFA----- )
     BEGIN
         DUP @        ( CFA(CFA)----- )
         80 AND 0=    ( CFA flag---- )
     WHILE
         1-           ( CFA-1----- )
     REPEAT
; <Return> OK
```

As this word has been defined, you can write

HEX ' NFA 2 - NFA <Return> 093A OK

093A is here the address of the string header of the word NFA. If you require less heavy use, you can easily define

```
: NAME HEX
      COMPILE  ' 2 -
      NFA DECIMAL
; IMMEDIATE <Return> OK
```

and you will then have

NAME NFA <Return> 093A OK

Bit 6 is the precedence bit.

This specifies for the interpreter the immediate character of the given word.

Note that IMMEDIATE forces to 1 the precedence bit of the last word created.

It is easy to build words capable of altering the precedence bit of any word in the dictionary.

```
: RESETPREC                   ( CFA--- )
          [COMPILE] NAME      ( NFA--- )
          DUP C@              ( NFA(NFA)--- )
          BF AND
          SWAP                ( (NFA)'NFA--- )
          C!
; <Return> OK

: SETPREC                     ( CFA--- )
        [COMPILE] NAME
        DUP C@
        40 OR
        SWAP
; <Return> OK
```

It is worth noting the essential difference between the word [COMPILE] and the word RESETPREC. The first does not affect the precedence bit, whereas the second has been written to set it at 0.

Bit 5 is the smudge bit.

This bit indicates to the interpreter the validity of the definition.

No doubt you have already encountered the problem of a non-valid definition.

This occurs when the interpreter refuses to compile a definition and gives an error message.

: TEST BEGIN ; <Return> MSG# 0 OK

The word is certainly present in the dictionary, as can be proved by VLIST, but any attempt to execute results in an error message (non-existent word).

The explanation is that, because of the sequential analysis of the definition, the word {:} has created a string header corresponding to this word, which VLIST can recognise. On the other hand, the interpreter has found a compiling anomaly and has therefore not cleared the smudge bit, which prevents all use of this embryo definition.

When the definition is correct, the word {;} takes charge of clearing this bit. If your definition does not terminate with {;}, when you use ;CODE for example, you should not forget to clear this bit immediately using the word SMUDGE.

The remaining bits 4,3,2,1,0 contain the length of the definition name.

6.2.2 Standard Defining Words

All words capable of creating a string header are called defining words. Up until now, we have met the following four such words

{:}, VARIABLE, CONSTANT and USER

All four create a string header with the same structure, as follows

A first byte, as described in section 6.2.1

A string of characters (ASCII code) containing the name of the word in which the MSB of its last byte is forced to 1.

A string pointer that points towards the preceding word of the current vocabulary.

To get gradually to grips with the subject of this chapter, we will look at the behaviour of the word CONSTANT.

Remember that a constant is defined thus

16 CONSTANT SIXTEEN <Return> <u>OK</u>

Its value is then read

SIXTEEN . <Return> <u>16 OK</u>

It is of course the execution of the word SIXTEEN which returns the value of the constant on the stack, without any compiling taking place (by means of {:}, for example).

If you look at the contents of the definition of SIXTEEN, you will only find the value 16 preceded by an address located at the CFA (figure 6.1).

In the light of your knowledge of the interpreter, you will know that when you type

SIXTEEN <Return> <u>OK</u>

the interpreter will execute the code pointed to by the CFA. It is therefore this execution that places the value of the constant on the stack.

This code, which the CFA of all constants point to, is in fact the second part of the definition of the word CONSTANT (the first part controls the string header). See figure 6.2.

The defining words that we shall now examine consist of two parts. The first part, which is executed when they are used to create a word, creates a string header. The second part is called when the words thus created are executed. They carry out the entire processing.

The advantage of such a tool is for example to be able to structure data. The method of handling will depend on the type of data involved.

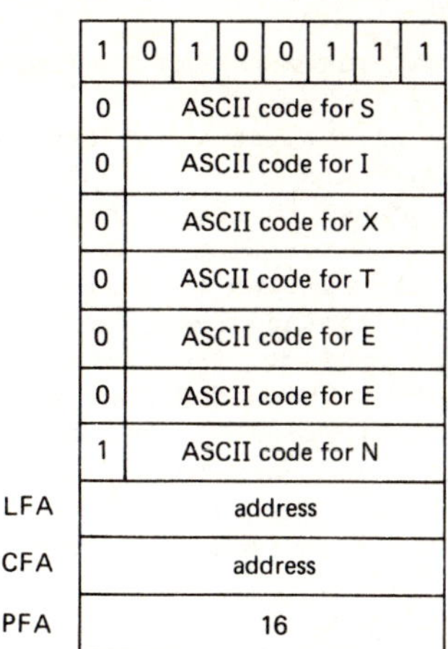

Figure 6.1

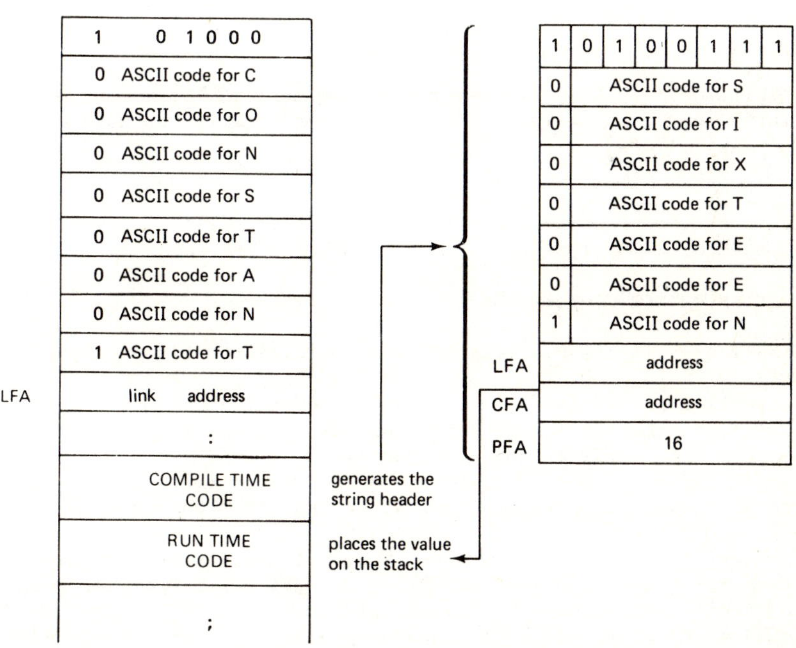

Figure 6.2

For constants, the process places the value of the constant on the stack. For variables, it places the address of the value on the stack (PFA).

Remember that for both constants and variables their value is at the PFA of the definition.

Knowing the addresses of the values of the variables, we can therefore easily alter them by means of the words {@} and {!}. As for the constants, we only have access to their values; it is this that makes it a more delicate task to alter them.

The User words are quite similar to variables in that they return the address of their value to the stack, but they are located in a different way in memory. In fact, the values are held in a table in a fixed location in memory. The address of the value in the table is found at the PFA of the definition of the User word.

The advantage of this fixed table becomes apparent when multitasking is implemented. The user variables are in fact the only words in basic FORTH that can be different from user to user.

6.2.3 Creating New Defining Words

The words involved here are <BUILDS and DOES>, always used as a pair. The general structure of the standard definition of a defining word takes the following form

```
: DEFININGWORD
               <BUILDS
                      Process 1
                DOES>
                      Process 2
; <Return> OK
```

<BUILDS effectively creates the string header. On execution of the defining word, the string header created will carry the name of the word that follows it.

Example

Suppose that we have defined the defining word DEFINE. After we have used the following syntax

```
DEFINE OBJECT <Return> OK
```

we shall find in the dictionary a new definition bearing the name OBJECT.

Execution of Process 1 takes place on execution of the definition word, after creation of the string header. We shall come to understand how this works in the next section.

The ultimate effect of defining words is to connect a given process (Process 2) with the execution of words that they have helped to define.

Process 2 is not to be executed when the definition word is executed (for example, DEFINE OBJECT). It must be appreciated that this process is resident in the defining word and not in that of the defined word, where it is only shown by a pointer, placed there by the execution of DOES>.

The function of DOES> is to direct the interpreter to Process 2 on execution of the defined word, after placing the PFA of the given word on the stack.

These details are sufficient for the creation and use of defining words. If you are curious to know the fundamentals of the problem, we shall look at the internal functioning of DOES>.

Let us go step by step through execution of the defined word OBJECT. We know that the interpreter will consider the contents of the definition of OBJECT as a sequence of CFAs of words to be executed. In our case, this method of functioning is not suitable if we think for example of the variables that contain a numerical value that is not a CFA. The word whose CFA is located at the CFA of OBJECT will therefore have to direct execution towards Process 2 and not towards the rest of the definition of OBJECT, at the same time placing the PFA+2 of OBJECT on the stack so that Process 2 knows where the call comes from.

The beginning of the definition of OBJECT therefore consists of two addresses: the CFA of the 'branching' word and the address of the jump, that is, the beginning of Process 2.

<BUILDS reserves two locations after the string header. Execution of DOES> will place the two 'pointer' addresses in these two memory locations.

Everything is therefore put together as shown in figure 6.3.

In fact, things are arranged more subtly still. The 'branching' word is included in the definition of DOES> and the correct arrangement is shown in figure 6.4.

We advise you to refer to the source of your own FORTH for fuller information.

As an application example, let us look at how we could write the defining words CONSTANT and VARIABLE in FORTH.

It is clear that the key is to find Process 1 and Process 2.

CONSTANT

Process 1	Process 2
Place the numerical value present on the stack in the first empty location in the dictionary (PFA+2)	With PFA+2 on the stack, find its contents and place them on the stack
That is, {,}	That is, {@}

```
: CONSTANT
        <BUILDS
                ,
         DOES>
; <Return> OK
```

VARIABLE

Process 1	Process 2
The same as for CONSTANT. That is, {,}	The begin address of the value is directly on the stack; there is therefore no additional processing.

```
: VARIABLE
        <BUILDS
                ,
         DOES>
; <Return> OK
```

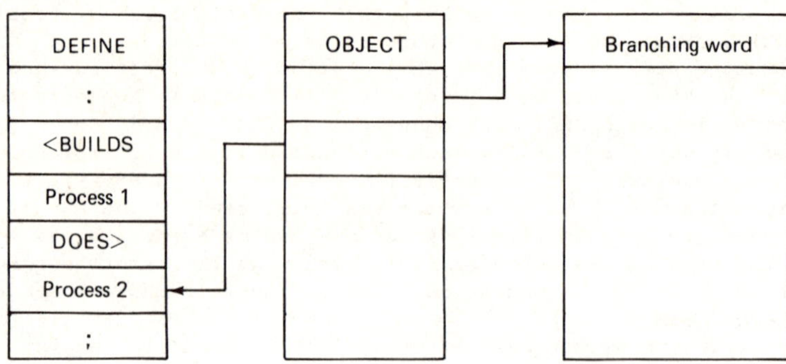

Figure 6.3

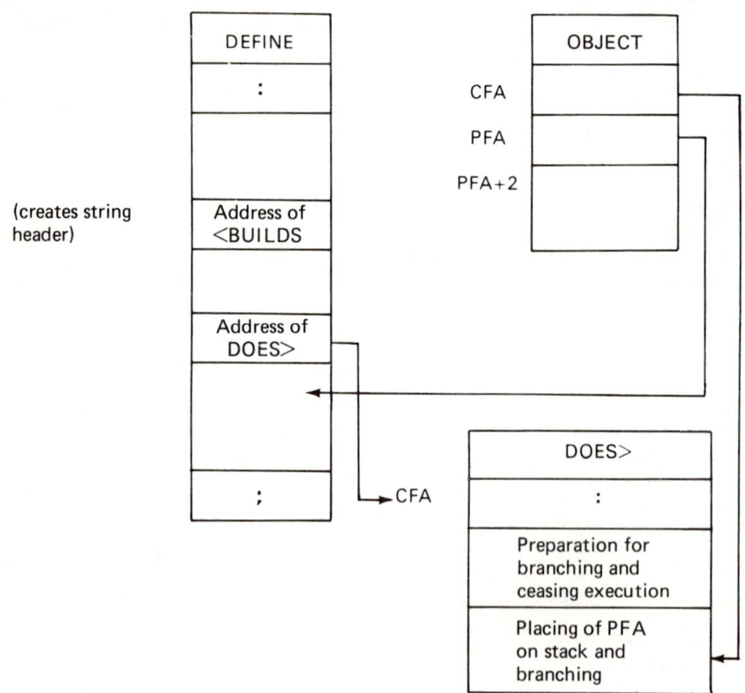

Figure 6.4

It is possible in the definition of a defining word to include an operation before <BUILDS. It will of course only be executed on execution of the defining word.

Example

```
: DEFINE
        ." I DEFINE"
        <BUILDS
                "Process 1"
         DOES>
                "Process 2"
; <Return> OK
```

On the other hand, it is not possible to nest <BUILDS and DOES> structures. In fact, DOES> calls upon the word LATEST in its execution which in turn returns the CFA of the last word of the current vocabulary, that is, the word being defined. We then arrive at the problem as shown in figure 6.5, in which the second DOES> does not operate on the good group of pointers.

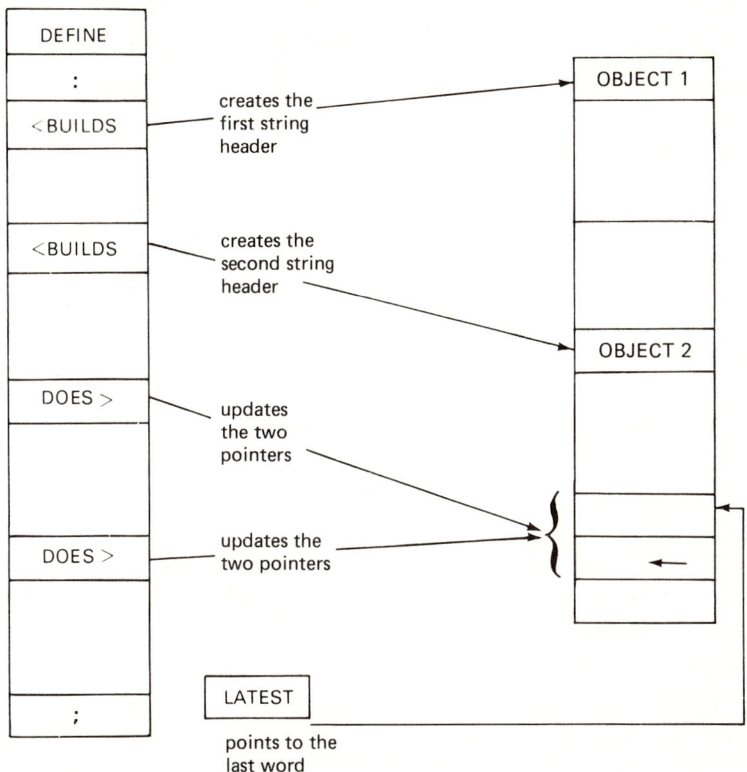

Figure 6.5

6.2.4 Using String and Array

The indispensable tool for creating complex data structures is ALLOT which reserves memory locations starting from the current position of the dictionary pointer (DP). It takes the number of bytes required from the stack and simply adds it to DP.

```
: ALLOT DP +! ; <Return> OK
```

ALLOT is not necessarily linked to the act of definition.

Strings

We now propose to implement in FORTH a character strings structure. This structure is to have standard features, as in BASIC, for example. The maximum capacity of the string is to be predefined. It must be capable of being accessed either in its entirety, or by means of a system of sub-strings.

For this, two indices are included in the definition; these are the maximum size of the string and the number of characters already assigned.

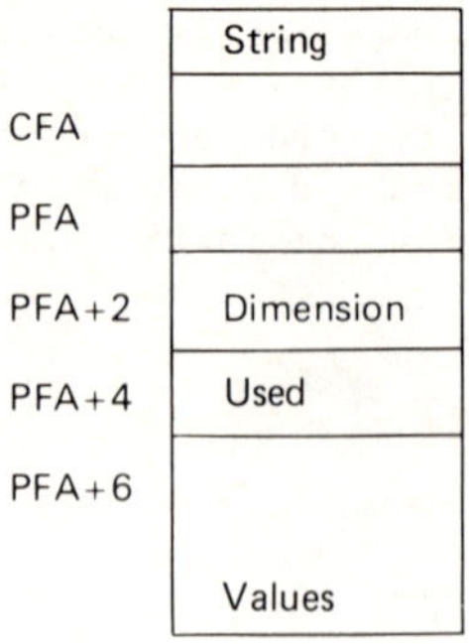

	String
CFA	
PFA	
PFA+2	Dimension
PFA+4	Used
PFA+6	Values

Figure 6.6

Our definition allows us to use the following syntax. For the string definition

Number of characters String String name

For access, execution of the string name will return to the stack

(-----String address Dimension used)

Implementation
The processing associated with <BUILDS will be

Take dimension from the stack and store it in the definition
Initialise to zero the number of characters used
Reserve the number of characters specified in the dimension.

The processing associated with DOES> consists in calculating and stacking the values required from PFA+2 that are present on the stack.

```
: STRING                  ( dim---- )
      <BUILDS
             DUP ,        ( dim--- ) stores the dimension
             0 ,          ( dim--- ) stores the number of characters
                                     used
             ALLOT        ( --- )    reserves the dimension
       DOES>
            DUP4 +SWAP  (String address Dimension address--- )
            DUP @ SWAP  (String dim. address Dimension address--- )
            2 + @       (String dim. address used-- )
; <Return> OK
```

To allocate a global value to this string, we have adopted a general method. The string will need to be marked off with quote marks in order to allow spaces to be included anywhere in the string.

It is useful to have a word available that finds a given character in memory, given a start address and an end address to limit the bounds of the search.

To achieve this the ASCII code of the character sought is placed on the stack, together with the begin address and the number of characters to be examined. After execution this word returns the address of the character sought, if it is found, together with a flag indicating success or failure.

```
: POS                         ( C Address Max---Flag address )
    0 SWAP                    ( C Address 0 Max--- )
    0 DO
        DROP                  ( C Address--- )
        OVER OVER @ - 0=      ( C Address flag --- )
        IF
          1 LEAVE             ( C Address 1--- )
        ELSE
           1 + 0              ( C Address+1 0--- )
        THEN
      LOOP
      ROT DROP                ( Address flag--- )
; <Return> OK
```

Starting with POS, we shall now construct a word that tests the validity of an alphanumeric constant between quotes, taking a begin address from the stack, being the maximum accepted length, and which, after testing, returns to the stack this same address, together with the effective length of the string and a flag indicating success or failure.

```
: ?STRING                        ( Address Max--- Address length flag )
        OVER C@                  ( Address Max C1--- )
                                   takes the first character)
        34 -                     ( Address Max flag--- )
        IF
          DROP 0 0               ( Address 0 0--- )
                                   does not begin with " )
          ." BAD SEPARATOR"
        ELSE
            OVER 34 ROT
                    ROT1         ( Address " Max Address--- )
            SWAP POS             ( Looks for second " )
        IF                       ( Address Address' --- )
          OVER - 1 - 1           ( Address length 1 --- )
        ELSE
            DROP 0 0             ( Address 0 )--- )
            ." STRING TOO LONG"
        THEN
THEN
; <Return> OK
```

We can now easily construct $=

```
: $=                                   ( Max address Used--- )
    DROP                               ( Max address--- )
    TIB @ IN @ +                       ( Max address Begin
                                         address--- )
    SWAP                               ( Address Begin address
                                         Max--- )
    ?STRING                            ( Address Begin address
                                         Length Flag--- )
    IF                                 ( Address Begin address
                                         Length--- )
      1 0 D+ ROT OVER OVER 2 - ! SWAP ( Updates used )
      THEN
      CMOVE QUIT
; <Return> OK
```

The three stages in realising $= take the following top-down form.

transfer a string from the terminal input buffer to the designated variable, then

test the validity of the next word as an alphanumeric constant, in terms of the presence of valid separators and whether the length does not exceed the maximum dimension, and then find a given character from a given start address memory, and within a limited search area.

Example

```
50 STRING TEST <Return> OK
TEST $= "STRING OF CHARACTERS" <Return> OK
```

From this point, it is very simple to display a string on the screen.

```
: $DISP                    ( Add Max Used --- )
       SWAP DROP TYPE
; <Return> OK
```

Similarly, the classic functions for string handling can be implemented as in the following examples.

Upper case to lower case

```
; $LWC                     ( Add Max Used --- )
      SWAP DROP            ( Add Used --- )
      0 DO                 ( Add --- )
          DUP C@           ( Add C --- )
          DUP 64 - 0>      ( test: is C an )
          OVER 91 - 0<     ( alphanumeric character? )
          *                ( Add C flag --- )
          32 * +           ( Add C+(flag*32) --- )
          OVER C! 1 +      ( Add+1 --- )
        LOOP
; <Return> OK
```

Lower case to upper case

```
: $UPC                     ( Add Max Used --- )
      SWAP DROP
      0 DO
          DUP C@
          DUP 96 - 0>
          OVER 123 - 0<
          *
          32 * -
          OVER C! 1 +
        LOOP
; <Return> OK
```

Arrays
Another example of the application of <BUILDS and DOES> is to implement two-dimensional matrices.

On creation of an array, the two dimensions are given. Access is either global or via a system of sub-matrices. For this, the table is included in the definition, preceded by two values corresponding to the two dimensions.

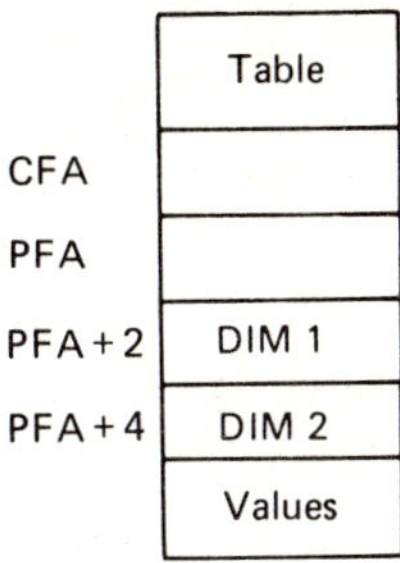

Figure 6.7

Our definition will allow us to use the following syntax. For setting up

```
DIM1 DIM2 MATDEF Array-name
```

For access, execution of

```
ind1 ind2 Array-name
```

will return to the stack the address of the designated element.

Implementation
The process associated with <BUILDS will be

a) to take the two dimensions from the stack and place them in the definition

b) to reserve dim1 × dim2 cells in the definition so that the matrix can subsequently be stored in them.

The process associated with DOES> consists in testing the validity of indices ind1 and ind2 in relation to dim1 and dim2, and then calculating the address of the element required by an arithmetic operation of the type

```
  PFA+6 + ( ind1 × Dim1 ) + ind2
: MATDEF                          ( Dim1 Dim2 --- )
        <BUILDS
             OVER OVER
             SWAP , ,
             * 2 * ALLOT
         DOES>                    ( Ind1 Ind2 PFA+2 --- )
              >R                  ( Ind1 Ind2 --- )
              OVER OVER           ( Ind1 Ind2 Ind1 Ind2 --- )
              R @                 ( Ind1 Ind2 Ind1 Ind2 Dim1 --- )
              R 2 + @             ( Ind1 Ind2 Ind1 Ind2 Dim1 Dim2 --- )
              ROT - 0>
              ROT
```

```
              ROT  -  0<       ( Ind1 Ind2 Flag1 Flag2 --- )
              *
              IF
                      R@ * + 2 *
                      R> 4 +          ( Offset PFA+6 --- )
                      +               ( Address --- )
              ELSE
                      R> DROP  DROP  DROP
                      ." BAD INDICES"
              THEN
   ; <Return> OK
```

From now on, each element of this two-dimensional matrix behaves individually like an ordinary variable, making reading and writing the elements as simple as in other languages.

To exploit this new data structure further, we can create the following simple word to display the contents of the whole array.

```
   : MATDISP
          [COMPILE] '            ( PFA --- )
           6 + DUP >R            ( CFA+8 --- )
             4 - @               ( CFA+8 Dim1 --- )
           R>  2 - @             ( CFA+8 Dim1 Dim2 --- )
           0 DO
               SWAP OVER         ( Dim1 Add Dim2 --- )
               0 DO
                    DUP @ .
                    2+
               LOOP
               SWAP              ( Add Dim1 --- )
           LOOP
           DROP DROP
   ; <Return> OK
```

It is used as MATDISP Array-name

6.3 EXECUTION BY INDIRECTION

We shall continue our discussion within the framework of the previous example.

In a number of elementary functions of matrix calculation there is always the same algorithm for scanning rows and columns. The only variation occurs at the heart of the two loops.

```
   : MATFN
        PREPARE                  ( PFA+6 dim1 dim2 --- )
        0 DO                     ( PFA+6 dim1 --- )
            SWAP OVER            ( dim1 PFA+6 dim1 --- )
            0 DO                 ( dim1 PFA+6 --- )
                DUP PROCESS 2 +
            LOOP
            SWAP                 ( PFA+6 dim1 --- )
        LOOP
        DROP DROP
   ; <Return> OK
```

with

```
: PREPARE
    [COMPILE] '          ( PFA --- )
     6 + DUP >R          ( PFA+6 --- )
     R 4 - @             ( PFA+6 dim1 --- )
     R> 2 - @            ( PFA+6 dim1 dim2 --- )
; <Return> OK
```

The word process, which has yet to be defined, represents one of a number of different possibilities.

The process for setting a constant value is written

```
: INIT
     CONST SWAP !
; <Return> OK
```

Similarly, the identity matrix will be generated automatically by the following process

```
: IDENT
    R> I J ROT >R
    = SWAP !
; <Return> OK
```

Note that the state of the return stack appears as shown in figure 6.8.

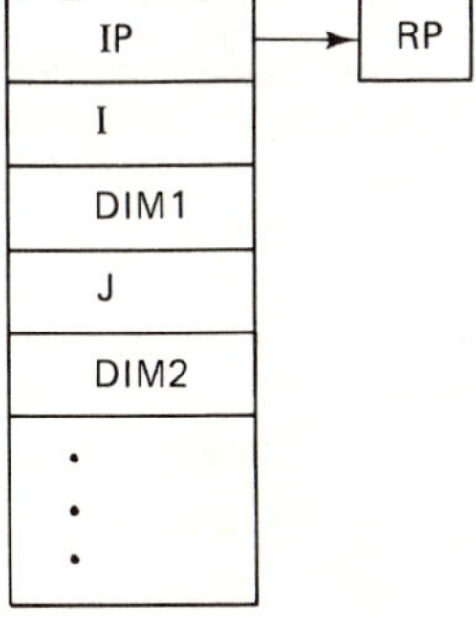

Figure 6.8

The top item is the return address for the word IDENT itself, and this explains why it is necessary to save the interpretation pointer in the data stack before being able to access I and J.

Scalar operations, such as adding the constant CONST to all elements, are written

```
: PLUS
     CONST OVER @ + SWAP !
; <Return> OK
```

The idea of execution by indirection is to be able to specify a process in an algorithm by means of a variable.

The basic tool to achieve this is the word EXECUTE which executes the word whose CFA is on the stack. We have already referred to it in our discussion of the internal mechanism of the interpreter in section 5.1.4.

There are two stages to putting into effect an execution by indirection (shown in figure 6.9)

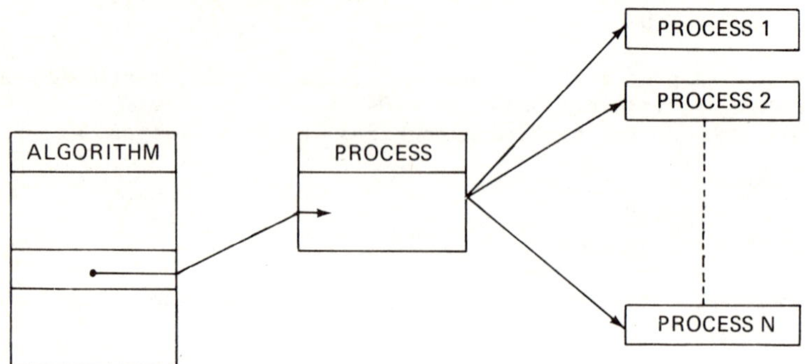

Figure 6.9

a) creation and preparation of a variable containing the CFA of the word corresponding to the chosen process.

b) replacement of the process in the algorithm by

```
PROCESS @ EXECUTE
```

We can see that this is an execution by indirection since it is possible to change the function of the algorithm by external means.

```
0 VARIABLE PROCESS
: MATFN
        PREPARE
        0 DO
             SWAP OVER
             0 DO
                  DUP PROCESS @ EXECUTE 2+
             LOOP
             SWAP
        LOOP
        2DROP
; <Return> OK
```

The functions are

```
: T-DISP ?  ; <Return> OK
: T-INIT CONST SWAP ! ; <Return> OK
: T-PLUS CONST OVER @ + SWAP ! ; <Return> OK
```

The corresponding processes are

```
: MATDISP ' T-DISP CFA CHANGE-PROCESS ! MATFN ; <Return> OK
: MATINIT ' T-INIT CFA CHANGE-PROCESS ! MATFN ; <Return> OK
: MATPLUS ' T-PLUS CFA CHANGE-PROCESS ! MATFN ; <Return> OK
```

In FORTH, it is always possible to work on two levels

a) either at the level of the traditional languages, in which case the functioning of the interpreter is transparent to the programmer;

b) or at a deeper and more powerful level, by integrating the application into the philosophy of the language.

6.4 SUMMARY

Word	*Syntax*	*Definition*
IMMEDIATE	IMMEDIATE	Makes the most recently defined word in the dictionary immediate, so that this word will itself be executed at the time of compilation of a definition in which it appears.
BRANCH	BRANCH "relative address"	Makes a branch to the relative address (that is, in relation to the position of BRANCH).
OBRANCH	OBRANCH "relative address"	Makes a conditional branch (zero flag on the stack) to the relative address (that is, in relation to the position of OBRANCH).
COMPILE	COMPILE "word"	On execution of the word whose definition contains COMPILE, the CFA of "word" will be read next from the dictionary.
[	["sequence of words"]	The interpreter goes into interpreter mode. This word is always used as a pair with].
]	["sequence of words"]	The interpreter returns to compilation mode. This word is always used after [.
[COMPILE]	[COMPILE] "word"	On compilation, the immediate word "word" is not executed but compiled. The interpreter takes no account of the value of its precedence bit.
C,	"byte" C,	The single byte value "byte" which precedes {C,} is read into the first free cell in the dictionary.
,	"value" ,	The two-byte value ("value") which precedes the word {,} is read into the first free cell in the dictionary.
<BUILDS	<BUILDS "Process1" DOES> "Process2"	The header of the process corresponding to compile-time. Always used as a pair with DOES>.
DOES>	<BUILDS "Process1" DOES> "Process2"	Marks the end of processing for compile-time and represents the header of the process ("Process2") corresponding to run-time. Always used as a pair with <BUILDS. After "Process2" no process can be interleaved before the end of definition word {;}.
ALLOT	"number" ALLOT	Reserves after the dictionary the specified number "number" of bytes.

6.5 EXERCISES

6.1 Define the words {,} and {C,} in FORTH using the word ALLOT.

6.2 Define the word COMPILE in FORTH.
Hint. The interpretive pointer on top of the return stack points to the next word after COMPILE in the definition currently being compiled.

6.3 Define in FORTH the words that make up the control structure IF ... ELSE ... THEN (or ENDIF).

7 Special Properties

7.1 VOCABULARIES

As we have already seen on several occasions, the dictionary is divided into vocabularies.

Each vocabulary takes the form of a linear string starting from the vocabulary name and continuing until it reaches a terminal leaf (see figure 7.1).

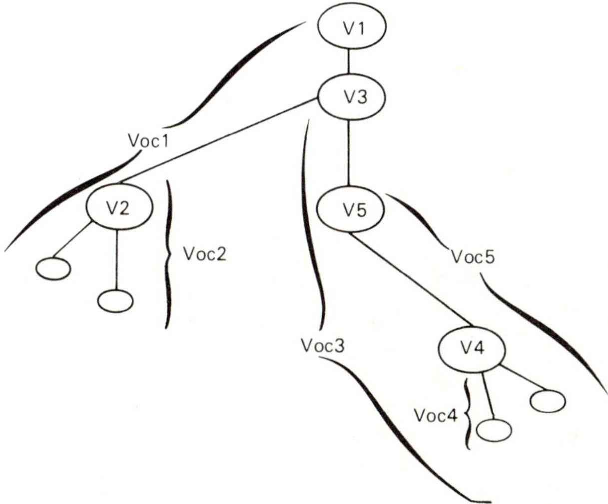

Figure 7.1

The search for a word in a vocabulary always begins at a leaf extremity and works back towards the root. It does not stop when it encounters the name of the vocabulary but continues back to the tree root. It is in this sense that one can appreciate that every vocabulary contains the core of FORTH.

This organisation is completely coherent with the structure of the definitions in the dictionary, since only a backward pointer is needed for its implementation, as shown in figure 7.2.

In order to create a vocabulary, the definition word VOCABULARY is used; working in the current vocabulary, it sets up a string header with the name of the new vocabulary. For example (see figure 7.3)

```
VOCABULARY VOC2 <Return> OK
```

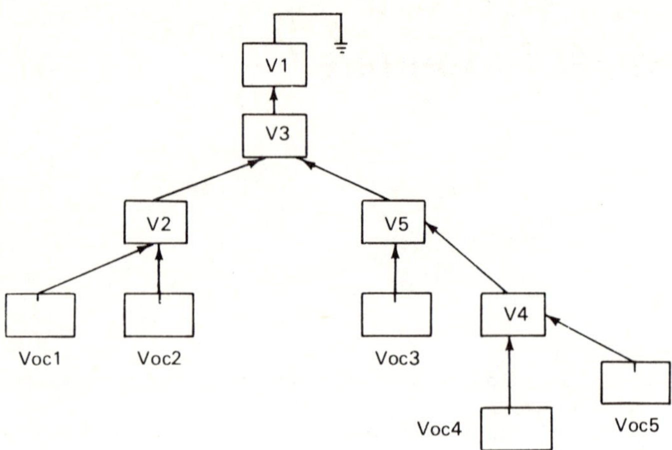

Figure 7.2

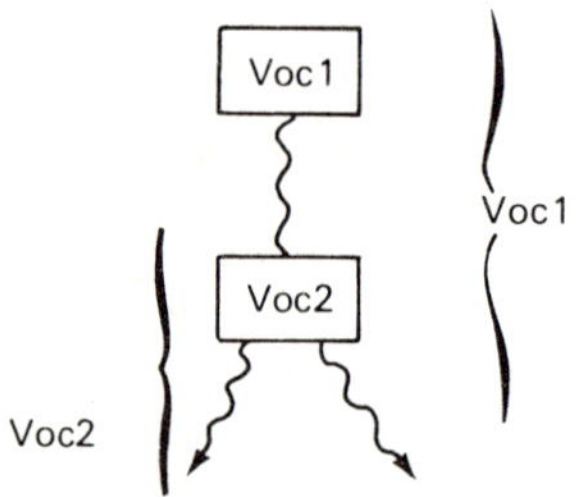

Figure 7.3

There is no limit to the number of vocabularies that can be created.

Each vocabulary has its corresponding string header whose address is simply stored in the definition of the vocabulary name. This is shown in figure 7.4.

These vocabularies can be used in two ways. They can either be used as the current (or definition) vocabulary, to which the new definitions will be added, or as the context vocabulary, in which case it is where the interpreter will search for the words that are submitted to it.

To put this concept into practice, two user variables are available - CURRENT and CONTEXT.

CURRENT points permanently to the zone of the definition zone of the current vocabulary that contains the NFA of the last word created in this vocabulary. This zone is situated at address PFA+4 of the VOCABULARY definition.

In order to find this NFA an indirection like CURRENT @ @ has to be used. This is the function of the word LATEST.

: LATEST CURRENT @ @ ; <Return> OK

With every new definition, CURRENT therefore remains unchanged.
Updating of the pointer to the last word created in the dictionary is done by an operation of the type CURRENT @ ! .
CONTEXT points to a similar zone, this time in the definition of the name of the context vocabulary.

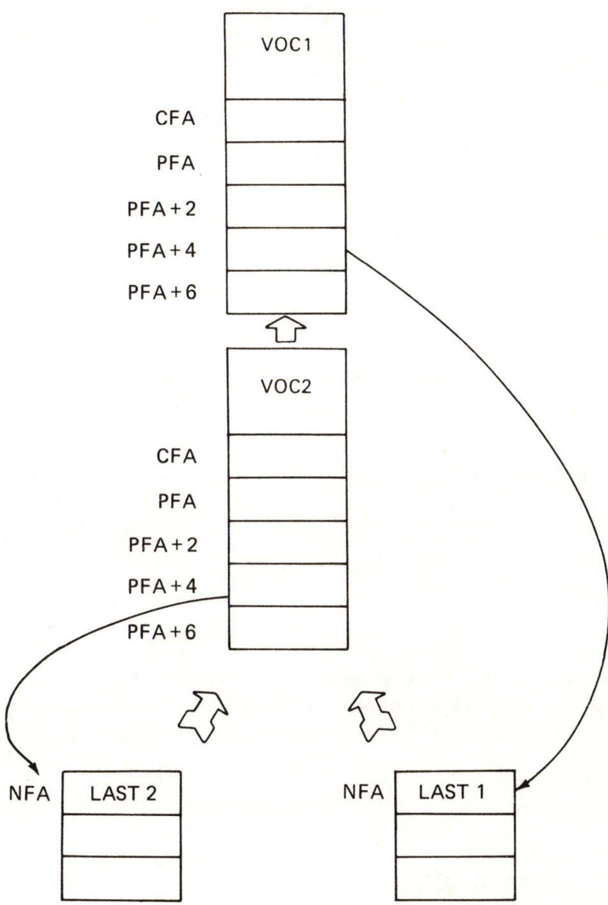

Figure 7.4

There is another feature of FORTH that enables the set of resident vocabularies to be known at any instant. To achieve this, the names of the different vocabularies are strung together in chronological sequence.
The head of this string is contained in the user variable VOC-LINK, which points to a zone situated at address PFA+6 in the definition of the name of the last vocabulary created.
This zone in turn points to the similar zone in the definition of the vocabulary name that chronologically precedes it, as shown in figure 7.5.

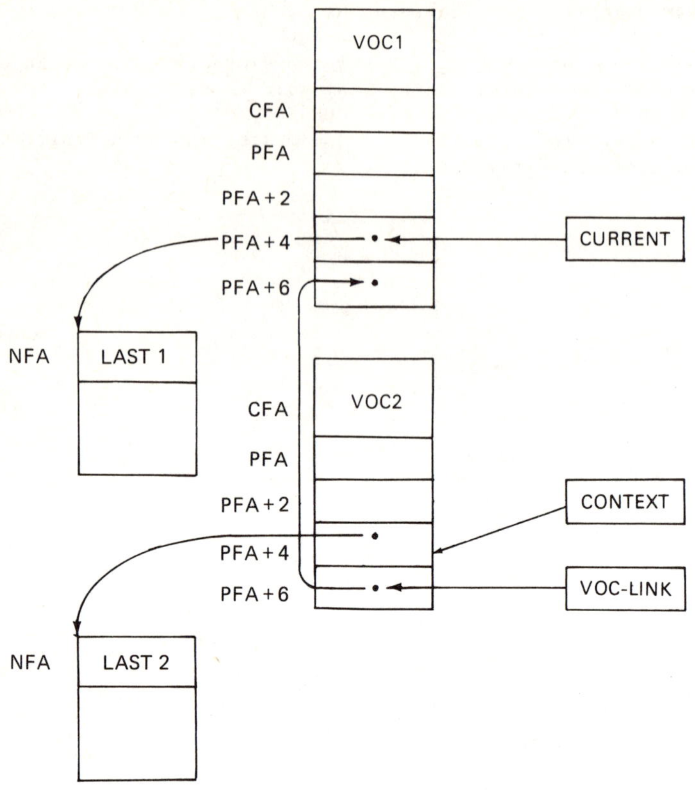

Figure 7.5

Although all the points have not yet been explained, we can nonetheless give you a definition of VOCABULARY to reinforce the concept. We shall review, element by element, the string header generated.

```
: VOCABULARY
    <BUILDS                  ( Creation of string header, filling of
                               CFA and PFA )
        A081 ,               ( Initialisation of PFA+2 )
        CURRENT @ CFA ,      ( Initialisation of PFA+4 )
        HERE VOC-LINK @ ,    ( Initialisation of PFA+6, and link to
                               the last created vocabulary )
        VOC-LINK   !         ( Updating of VOC-LINK )
    DOES>                    ( Places the PFA on the stack on ex-
                               ecution of the word )
        2+  CONTEXT  !       ( Makes CONTEXT point to the chosen
                               vocabulary )
; <Return> OK
```

On seeing this definition, your first question could well be about the function of the 81A0 placed at address PFA+2 of the generated definition. (Note: most processors store the low byte first.)

Those rare works that do attempt to explain 81A0 describe it as a 'dummy header'. In fact, 81A0 corresponds to figure 7.6.

1 S P -----L-----

1	0	0	0	0	0	0	1	81
1	0	1	0	0	0	0	0	A0

Msb Lsb

Figure 7.6

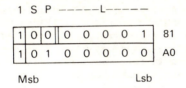

These two bytes can therefore be seen as the string header of a word whose name is a space character. This is effectively how the interpreter understands it, and we now need to explain its function.

Suppose that our FORTH appears as represented in figure 7.7.

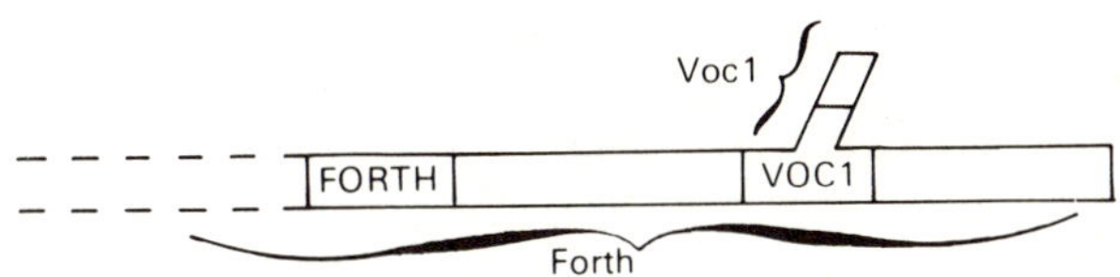

Figure 7.7

At some stage, you have created VOC1, together with a certain number of definitions under this vocabulary. Then, again in FORTH, you have created other words. If you now place yourself in VOC1 and type VLIST on your terminal, you will see the definitions appear in the following order

Definitions made under VOC1

(three spaces)

Definitions made under FORTH

VOC1

Remaining definitions

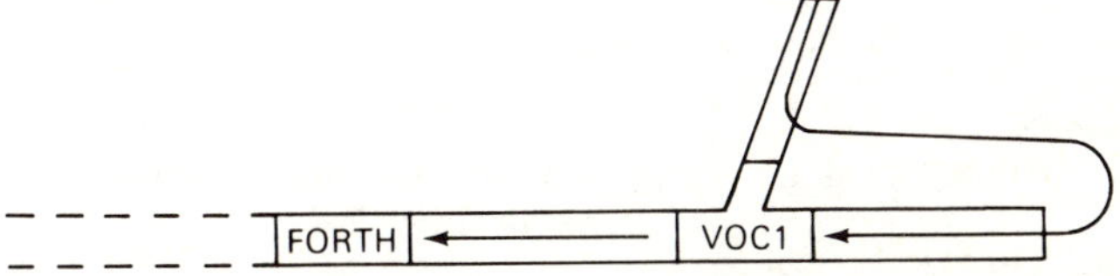

Figure 7.8

The tree has been followed in an unexpected way (figure 7.8).

With the knowledge that VLIST only follows the chaining of the LFAs until it finds one that is null, we can postulate two possible explanations.

Either the LFA of the first word created in VOC1 points to the NFA of the last word created using FORTH. This assumes that each new word created using FORTH requires this LFA to be updated.

Or, knowing that in the definition of the FORTH vocabulary the contents of the cell with address PFA+4 always points to the NFA of the last word created in this vocabulary, it is sufficient to take this cell as a LFA and to make the LFA of the first word in VOC1 point to the NFA of a corresponding dummy word. The chain would then be complete, the dummy name header being none other than 81A0.

Figure 7.9 shows a more complete representation.

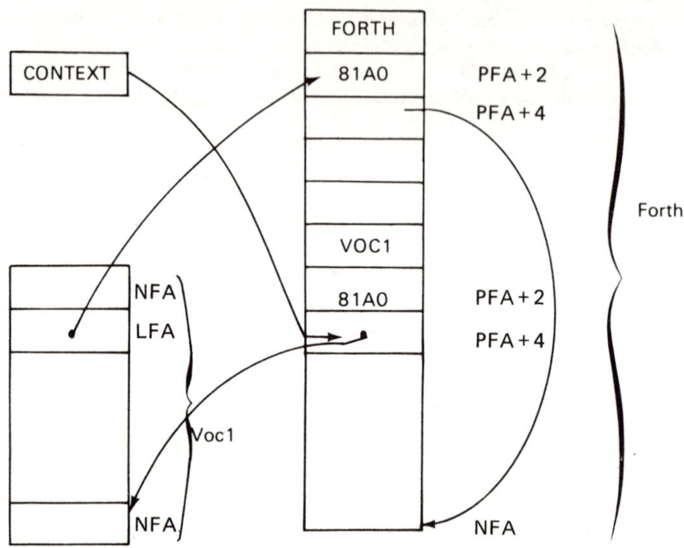

Figure 7.9

Every dictionary search begins at the address obtained by executing CONTEXT @ .

We are therefore at the dummy word of the context vocabulary. Its LFA points to the NFA of the last word in the vocabulary.

For the first word created in VOC1, its LFA points to the NFA of the dummy word in the vocabulary in which VOC1 was created.

One can trace the movement via these dummy string headers in VLIST; they appear as spaces.

Shown below is the algorithm path for VLIST; incidentally, it is the same for any dictionary search.

```
: SEARCH
        CONTEXT @ @       ( NFA of last word created in the context
                            vocabulary )
        BEGIN
              DUP         ( NFA NFA --- )
              PROCESSING  ( Must use up a NFA )
              PFA         ( PFA --- )
              LFA         ( LFA --- )
               @          ( (LFA)--- )
              DUP         ( (LFA)(LFA)--- )
              0=          ( (LFA) flag--- )
```

```
        UNTIL
        DROP
  ; <Return> OK
```

The direct application is VLIST, in which the processing to be carried out consists in making a transfer down the line and editing the name of the word.

```
  : PROCESSING
        OUT @          ( Gives the number of characters sent )
        C/L            ( Gives the number of characters/line )
        >
        IF
             CR        ( Transfer to the line )
             0 OUT !   ( Resets character counter )
        ENDIF
        ID.            ( Displays the name from NFA )
        SPACE
  ; <Return> OK
```

We now return to the contents of the definition of VOCABULARY. The sequence

```
  A081
  CURRENT @ CFA ,
```

can be divided into two operations

Creation of the dummy string header

Initialisation of the LFA of this dummy string header. It is made to point to the NFA of the dummy word in the current vocabulary, under which this new vocabulary is created. (As we have already seen, the action of the word CFA is 2-.)

These actions can be portrayed as shown in figure 7.10.

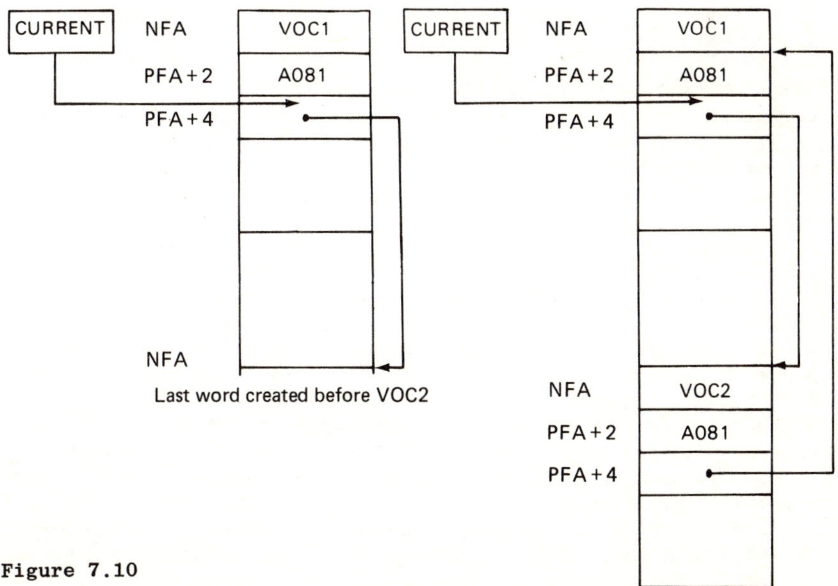

Figure 7.10

The following sequence

```
HERE VOC-LINK @ ,
VOC-LINK !
```

enables VOC2 to be introduced in the parallel chaining of the vocabularies (see figure 7.11).

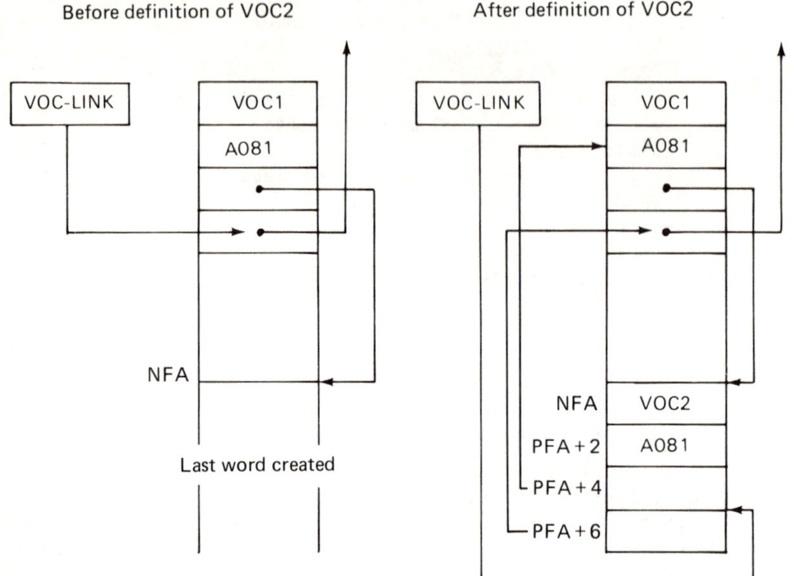

Figure 7.11

The following sequence executed on calling the vocabulary name

```
2+ CONTEXT !
```

makes CONTEXT point to the address element PFA+4 in the vocabulary definition. This vocabulary then becomes the context vocabulary.

If no word has yet been defined in this vocabulary, this zone points to the dummy chain header in the 'father' vocabulary definition. If words have been defined, it points to the last word defined in the vocabulary in question.

We now take a closer look at what happens when the first word is created in VOC2, with VOC2 being the current vocabulary.

The interpreter goes to look for the NFA of the last defined word in the definition of VOC2, at address PFA+4; this NFA will be the contents of the LFA of the word being defined. It will subsequently place in the element of address PFA+4 in the definition of VOC2, the NFA of the word that has just been defined.

When we come to creating the first word of VOC2, this general process will have the effect of initialising the contents of the LFA of VOC2 towards the NFA of the dummy string header of the 'father' vocabulary of VOC2.

It now remains to see how to move into a given (current) definition vocabulary. This is done by using the word DEFINITIONS which is defined

```
: DEFINITIONS
        CONTEXT @
        CURRENT !
; <Return> OK
```

This word turns the context vocabulary into the current vocabulary. So, in order to make a vocabulary current, we must first make it the context vocabulary.

Example

```
VOC2 DEFINITIONS <Return> OK
```

The act of typing VOC2 makes VOC2 the context vocabulary, while typing DEFINITIONS makes the current vocabulary identical to the context vocabulary (here VOC2).

When using FORTH in a professional application, it is crucial for the user only to have access to a limited vocabulary of high-level words that are specific to his needs.

One starts with the assumption that the user only has the possibility to type the key words of his application.

To achieve this all that is necessary is for these words to be grouped in the same vocabulary which is made the context vocabulary; then, the link that connects the first word of this specific vocabulary to its father vocabulary is broken.

From then on, the interpreter will only search in this isolated branch.

In other circumstances, it is often useful in definitions to call words resident in vocabularies that have no related link.

Here the only course of action is to make the vocabularies in question immediate. Remember that the word IMMEDIATE only acts on the last word created. It will therefore be necessary to make the vocabularies immediate as soon as they are created.

Example
VOC1 and VOC2 have been declared immediate. Suppose we are in VOC2 as the current and context vocabulary, and we want to define a word TEST2 which uses the word TEST1 defined in VOC1.
The solution is as follows

```
: TEST2 ----- VOC1 TEST1 VOC2 --- ;
```

As VOC1 is immediate, on finding it the interpreter has made it the context vocabulary and has therefore recognised the word TEST1. Return to the initial context vocabulary is undertaken by VOC2. This is only possible because the two vocabularies are immediate.

7.2 SEGMENTATION

As Meyer has put it very well: 'The programmer's basic task is to disregard at every level all irrelevant details, extract that which can be left until later, in order to be able to concentrate solidly on the main problems.'

Each of these levels of abstraction represents a logical layer in the decomposition of the problem.

Example
We can break down the problem of the display of all the words in the current vocabulary (VLIST), as shown in figure 7.12.

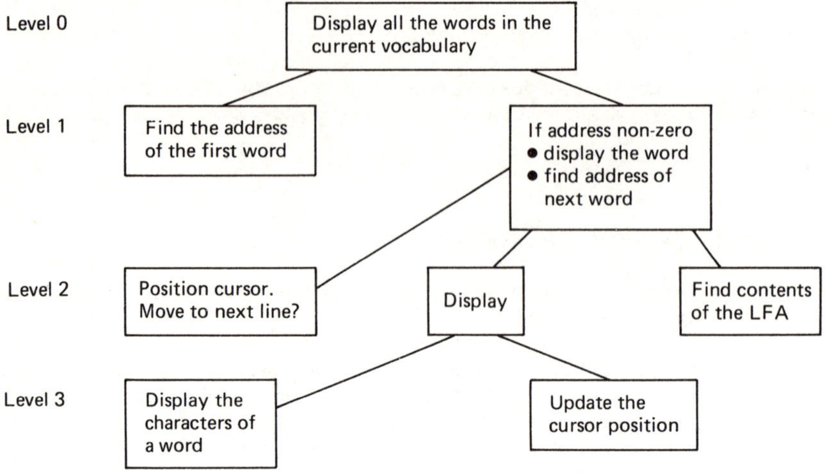

Figure 7.12

Note that the interest of this breakdown is closely dependent on three criteria: the complexity of the problem, the development level of the programming tool and the skill of the programmer.

Once the principle of breaking down a problem into its logical levels has been adopted, one is then faced with the question of which order to approach the levels in.

Two methods suggest themselves of their own accord. One can successively break things down until one reaches a problem level where the problems can be solved by a programming language. This is the top-down approach.

Alternatively, using tools built up brick by brick, one can climb towards the global problem, relying at each stage on the results already achieved. This is the bottom-up approach.

This last concept is in fact only affectively applicable on the basis of an extensive breakdown of the problems, which can then be regrouped into families in order to construct tools that are more particularly suited to the task in hand.

Problems presented by the top-down approach
The initial choices that are made at the highest levels are crucial. It is very difficult to re-examine them without having to redo the analysis completely.

The tree produced can conceal similarities between sub-trees. This is why it is always advisable to follow up a top-down analysis with a synthesis in order to shed light on the general character of certain problems.

Problems presented by the bottom-up approach
Experience shows that a bottom-up synthesis leads one to exaggerate the hypothesis used to construct different modules.

The interfaces then become too difficult to manipulate. This can lead to a catastrophe when one remembers that in FORTH it is beyond the powers of humans to manipulate more than four or five items in the stack.

Furthermore, there is no certainty that incompatibilities will not be found between problems to be solved and modules already constructed, which inevitably casts doubt on the general applicability of these tools.

What can we learn in FORTH from these general concepts?

FORTH ensures that the definition of words cannot exceed a certain size without introducing an unacceptable difficulty. Therefore, the modules that are employed in the solution of a problem must be short and deliberately selected.

One of the limitations to segmentation in conventional languages is the difficulty of interfacing between modules (parameter declarations). FORTH solves this problem by providing, in addition to variables, a data stack.

FORTH optimises the memory space occupied by the different modules. There is no transfer of parameters in the traditional sense; the non-active part of the code corresponding to each module is limited to its simplest means of expression, that is, the string header.

One might consider FORTH to be restricted by the types of parameter transfer between modules that it allows. However, we think that such focusing on the transfer of parameters is only the fruit of bad analytic habits in the older languages. They tend to obscure the global legibility of the program and pander to any tendency to laziness on the part of the programmer.

If you analyse problems soundly, you will never be confounded by them.

An important factor in perfecting a programming method is the correct use of tests.

Experience teaches that beyond a certain level of complexity, the work load represented by tests is considerable. The results are often imperfect, because it is not always easy to test all cases.

Top-down analysis by logic layers leads naturally to a systematic method of logical tests.

In any given layer, the elements at a lower level, even if not written down, are nonetheless specified functionally.

So, in order to test the element that will make use of them, they can be replaced by temporary frameworks that can at least in part carry out simple operations that conform to the functional specification, but without relating to the problem to be dealt with.

To illustrate this, let us examine a concrete example. Take the task of listing on a printer a simple file while ensuring correct page control. The printer is only to move to a new page when the current page is full.

The first algorithm that we put forward is known to be incorrect.

```
: LIST
      CR
      PAGE           ( Top-of-page, reset line counter, set
                       header )
      BEGIN
           N-EOF     ( Test for end of file )
      WHILE
           READ      ( Read a record )
           DISPLAY   ( Print it )
           INCREMENT ( Increment line counter )
           TEST      ( Test the number of lines per page )
           IF
```

```
                    F-PAGE ( Produce page footer )
                    PAGE
                THEN
        REPEAT
        F-PAGE
    ; <Return> OK
```

The 'thinking' points in this algorithm occur in the behaviour of N-EOF and TEST.

Here are the fictitious definitions that we shall give to the other words, without touching a comma of the definition of LIST.

```
: PAGE 0 LINE ! ." HEAD " CR ; <Return> OK
: F-PAGE ." FOOT  "  CR ; <Return> OK
: READ ; <Return> OK
: EDIT LINE @ . CR ; <Return> OK  ( LINE contains the line number )
: INCREMENT LINE 1 +! ; <Return> OK
```

In order to test the algorithm thoroughly, it is necessary to examine its behaviour using all possible values, that is

1)	N-EOF value 0	The behaviour of TEST is not of interest to us because we do not re-enter the loop.
2)	N-EOF value 1	TEST takes the value 0 a certain number of times, then takes the value 1.
3)	TEST value 0	N-EOF changing from 1 to 0.
4)	TEST value 1	N-EOF changing from 1 to 0.

It is not possible for N-EOF to change from 0 to 1 owing to the structure of the sequential files.

Case 1

```
: N-EOF 0 ; <Return> OK
LIST <Return>
HEAD
FOOT OK
```

This shows that an empty file still causes a page to be edited. It is just as well to know this.

Case 2

```
: N-EOF 1 ; <Return> OK
: TEST LINE @ 5 = ; <Return> OK
LIST <Return>
HEAD
1
2
3
4
FOOT
HEAD
1
.
.
OK
```

The move to the next page is correctly executed.

Case 3

```
: TEST 0 ; <Return> OK
5 VARIABLE CAN <Return> OK
: NEOF CAN DUP 1-  +STORE @ 5 / ; <Return> OK
LIST <Return>
HEAD
1
2
3
4
FOOT
OK
```

The end of the file is correctly indicated.

Case 4

```
: TEST 1 ; <Return> OK
LIST <Return>
HEAD
1
2
3
4
FOOT
HEAD
FOOT
OK
```

Here we have an incorrect page jump that we should never have detected without using this systematic checking procedure.

It is what happens when the page jump resulting from the line count coincides exactly with the end of the file.

In fact, the correct algorithm is as follows

```
: LIST
     CR
     PAGE
     BEGIN
          N-EOF
     WHILE
          TEST
          IF
               F-PAGE
               PAGE
          THEN
          READ
          DISPLAY
          INCREMENT
    REPEAT
    F-PAGE
; <Return> OK
```

If this method is followed systematically, it has the advantage of ensuring that the whole process is tested, layer by layer.

At the same time, it will be seen that building such scaffoldings can be a difficult and non-trivial task. The best means of eliminating quickly those cases that are perfectly obvious (or quite impossible!) is by carrying out a thorough initial analysis.

7.3 RECURSION

Recursion is concerned with the possibility of including in the definition of an object, a reference to that same object.

This concept of object is very broad.

Mathematical formulae

Factorial functions

0! = 1
N! = N * (N-1)!   for all N > 0

Combinatory functions

$C_n^o = 1$ for integer n

$C_n^m = 0$ for integer m and n, m > n

$C_n^m = C_{n-1}^{m-1} + C_{n-1}^m$ for integer m and n, m <= n

Data structures

Binary tree
type Binary-Tree = (Empty : Non-Empty-Binary-Tree)
type Non-Empty-Binary-Tree = (root:T;ℓst,rst:Binary-Tree)
rst: right sub-tree   ℓst: left sub-tree

In the first two examples, recursion is direct; that is, the recursive call to the object occurs within the very definition of the object. This is not always the case, as is shown by the definition of the binary trees.

For the uninitiated reader, the concept of recursion will perhaps seem to be nothing more than an intellectual game whose solution is lost in an infinite number of recursive calls.

It is therefore no surprise to learn that an essential condition in the use of recursion is that the objects generated must be finite. Thus, every group of recursive definitions will necessarily have to contain a clause specifying that, in certain cases, evaluation may occur without recourse to recursion.

Another determining condition in the success of a recursive definition is the presence of a control quantity which is guaranteed to converge strictly at each recursion call.

Example

In the factorial function case, the control quantity is the argument itself, and the immediate evaluation clause is 0!=1.

In the binary tree case, the control quantity is the height of the tree, and the immediate evaluation clause is EMPTY.

FORTH and recursion

At first sight, FORTH appears to contain no direct possibility of supporting recursion. For example, try to define

```
: OBJECT OBJECT ; <Return> OBJECT Msg#0   OK
```

The interpreter will not accept this definition because it has looked in the vocabulary for a valid definition of the words that go to make it up; that is, the word OBJECT. The string header of OBJECT certainly exists (created by {:}), but it has not yet been validated (when {;} is reached).

The most elegant solution is to validate OBJECT manually before the recursion call, by using the word SMUDGE which is most conveniently immediate.

Example

```
: FACT
      SMUDGE
      IF
        DUP 1 - FACT*
      ELSE
        1
      THEN
; <Return> OK
```

This time the definition will be accepted by the interpreter. Now try typing 3 FACT, for example, to execute it.

An error message will appear saying that there is no valid definition of FACT!

To understand this response, it should be remembered that SMUDGE only complements the Smudge bit (definition validity bit) in the string header of the last definition created.

It is the same when {;} validates a definition. The two successive complementations then cancel each other out.

We therefore only need to introduce an additional complementation by incorporating a second SMUDGE at the end of the definition.

The correct definition of FACT is then

```
: FACT
      SMUDGE
      IF
          DUP 1 - FACT *
      ELSE
          1
      THEN
      SMUDGE
; <Return> OK
```

As we have just seen, embedding direct recursive structures in FORTH is very easy.

There is another more complicated way of doing this; it involves reserving two bytes in the definition of the recursive word.

Subsequently, the CFA of the word in question will be stored in this reserved space, so that the definition can be made recursive.

To do this, the recursive reference is replaced by a fictitious word, NOOP, chosen because it has no action at all.

```
: NOOP ; <Return> OK
```

Now that the definition is validated, the operator calls the word RECURSE which goes to look for the CFA of the last word defined and substitutes it for the CFA of NOOP in the definition.

This type of method allows indirect recursive structures to be embedded. In the final chapter we shall develop two classic recursive algorithms - the towers of Hanoi and the eight queens.

One of the obstacles to embedding recursion in high-level languages is the transfer of parameters when procedures are called. The problem posed in controlling the recursion lies in saving, at each call, the data necessary for continuation of execution at level n, after return from level n-1.

It must therefore be possible for the contexts corresponding to each level to be called in inverse order from that in which they were saved. We can see that a typical LIFO stack structure will allow such memory saves and successive calls. This is one of the reasons why the majority of high-level recursive languages use stacks, like FORTH.

7.4 MULTITASKING

FORTH belongs to a family of languages capable of controlling several simultaneous tasks without the aid of an external operating system.

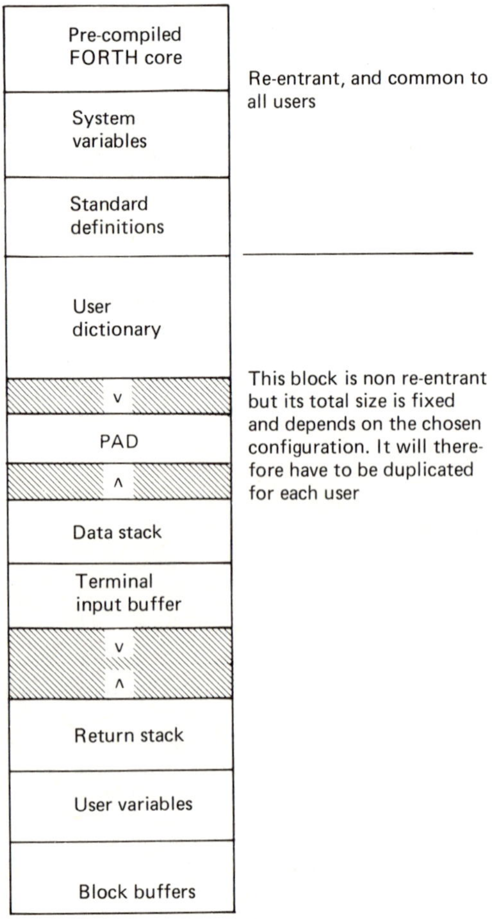

Figure 7.13

In the case of the traditional languages, the solution of this problem is delegated to a machine control program, which is usually supplied by the manufacturer.

The possibility of multitasking is of considerable interest to microcomputer users, since this is a hitherto rarely offered facility. The reasons for this have been the often small amounts of free memory available for storing an operating system and a language at the same time, together with the slowness of mass storage.

With FORTH, we have the following advantages.

The basic core of FORTH, which is purely re-entrant, can be divided into N simultaneous tasks. Its utilisation rate is considerable, since the execution of every FORTH word inevitably ends up there.

The memory allocation for each task is dynamic. All the words that make up the different applications are stored sequentially in memory, and they are linked by vocabularies thanks to the strings maintained by the interpreter. In addition, the word definitions are extremely compact. A complete, well-written FORTH application occupies less space than if it had been written in assembler.

It is quite feasible to envisage five tasks going on simultaneously in 48K of FORTH, in a standard 8-bit microcomputer configuration.

There is no intention in this section to go into the details of the implementation of multitasking. The control of non-shareable resources, for example, lies outside the scope of this book. We shall simply highlight the broad principles.

There is a 'super FORTH' called polyFORTH which can, among other things, be multitasked and has been made available commercially for many machines.

Figure 7.13 shows a single-user FORTH memory map.

In a multi-user system, there would be the need for secondary tasks going on in the background. The memory map for such tasks might appear as in figure 7.14.

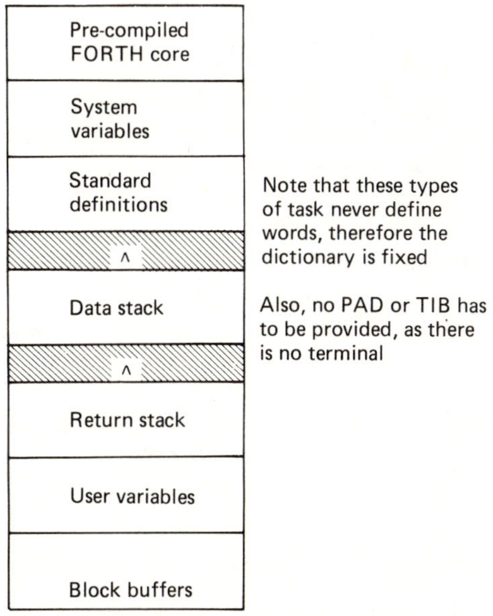

Pre-compiled FORTH core
System variables
Standard definitions
^
Data stack
^
Return stack
User variables
Block buffers

Note that these types of task never define words, therefore the dictionary is fixed

Also, no PAD or TIB has to be provided, as there is no terminal

Figure 7.14

In order to be able to configure dynamically the size of the memory areas allocated to each task, it would be practical to fix on one user to play the role of operator.

The most natural configuration for a multi-user system will therefore be as shown in figure 7.15. Note that the block buffers are shared in order to facilitate control of the sharing of mass storage.

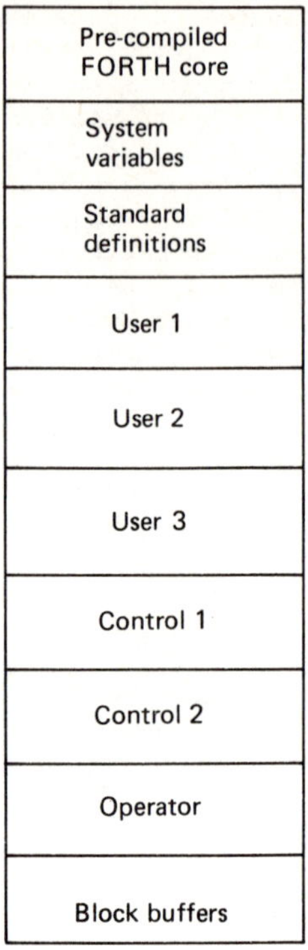

Pre-compiled FORTH core
System variables
Standard definitions
User 1
User 2
User 3
Control 1
Control 2
Operator
Block buffers

Figure 7.15

7.5 SUMMARY

Word	*Syntax*	*Definition*
VOCABULARY	VOCABULARY "voc"	Definition word of a vocabulary whose name is "voc"
DEFINITIONS	"voc"DEFINITIONS	As the context vocabulary is "voc" (as soon as voc is typed), the current vocabulary also becomes "voc"
SMUDGE	SMUDGE	Complements the smudge bit of the last word created.

8 Problems

In this chapter, we propose to solve some simple problems in FORTH in order to make you more familiar with the language.

The list of problems is as follows

1. Manipulation of complex numbers
2. Life game (Conway's Universe)
3. Trigonometric functions
4. The towers of Hanoi
5. The eight Queens (recursion)
6. Perpetual Gregorian calendar
7. Sequential files

8.1 COMPLEX NUMBERS AND THEIR MANIPULATION

Mathematics revision

A complex number is in fact a pair of real numbers on which the following operations are authorised

```
                    c1 :=(a1,b1)                 c2 :=(a2,bs)
complex addition   c1+c2 :=(a1+a2,b1+b2)
  scalar multiplication
by a real number   s.c1 :=(s.a1,s.b1)
  complex multiplication
                         c1*c2 :=(a1.a2 - b1.b2,a1.b2 + a2.b1)
```

There is no need to extend the mathematical properties of this group further. We note simply that it is convenient to represent a complex number in the following way

c := a+ib

where i is the complex square root of -1, that is

i*i = -1

The set of complex numbers is a two-dimensional vector space with base vectors 1 and i.

We may also define the conjugate of a complex number, that is, another complex number that is symmetrical to the first about the real axis. Thus

c := a+ib

has the (complex) conjugate c' := a-ib. Note that if c lies on the real axis (that is b = 0), then c and c' are coincident.

Similarly, the term 'modulus' is used to describe the size of a complex number

$|c| := (a.a+b.b)^{\frac{1}{2}}$

This represents geometrically the length of the real vector

v = (a,b)

Given that i*i = -1, it will be seen that $|c|^2 = c*c'$.

Continuing with these geometrical analogies, the 'argument' of a complex number is naturally introduced, corresponding to the angle of the real vector with the vector (1,0)

arg(c) = arctan(b/a)

We may then write

c := |c|.(cos(arg(c)) + i sin(arg(c)))

Taylor expansion

The Taylor expansion of e^{ix} is

$$e^{ix} = 1 + ix + \frac{(-1)x^2}{2!} + \frac{(i)x^3}{3!} + \ldots$$

$$= (1 - \frac{x^2}{2!} + \frac{x^4}{4!} \ldots) + i(x - \frac{x^3}{3!} + \frac{x^5}{5!} \ldots)$$

$$= \cos x + i \sin x$$

thus

$$c = |c| . (\cos x + i \sin x) = |c| \; e^{ix}$$

Note the following properties of the 'modulus' and 'argument' functions

$|c1*c2| = |c1|.|c2|$
$|c1+c2| \leqslant |c1|+|c2|$
arg(c1*c2)= arg(c1) + arg(c2)

This last property is interesting, since it will allow us to extend the concept of real exponential to that of complex exponential, given that it is usual to write

c = d.(sin(x)+i.cos(x)) = d exp(ix)

where d = |c| and x = arg(c).

The task is to generate the data structure 'complex number', in fixed point, having the following application operators

addition, subtraction
multiplication by a real number
multiplication of two complex numbers
modulus
argument
conjugate

8.1.1 Generation of Complex Numbers

As one might expect, we need to use the definition tools of definition words to solve this first step.

The new data structure that interests us has the following characteristics.

Each item simply comprises two real numbers, as a consequence of the real plane and the complex plane.

Access to each complex variable is via its name, which has the effect of returning to the stack the address of the imaginary component, with the real component following it into the memory.

The syntax for the creation of a complex variable is

```
RP IM COMPLEX name-of-variable
```

where RP is the real part and IM the purely imaginary part.

The definition word for the definition of complex variables then becomes

```
: COMPLEX
      <BUILDS
            (stores the two values at the top of the stack one
             after the other in the dictionary)
      ' '
      DOES>
            (the required address is already on the stack)
;
<Return> OK
```

We can now write

```
1 2 COMPLEX ONE-TWO <Return> OK
```

The structure generated can be shown as follows

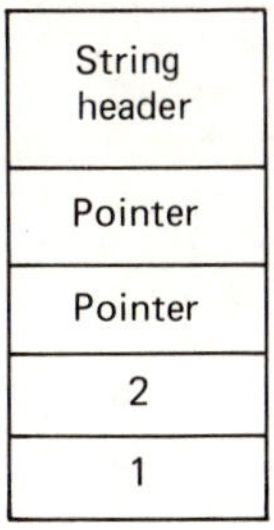

String header
Pointer
Pointer
2
1

We can now make use of this tool to access the values of the complex variables

```
: X@            ( addr ... re im )
     DUP        ( addr addr ... )
     @          ( addr im ... )
     SWAP       ( im addr ... )
     2+         ( im addr+2 ... )
     @          ( im re ... )
     SWAP       ( re im ... )
; <Return> OK
```

```
: X!            ( re im addr ... )
    SWAP OVER ! 2+ !
; <Return> OK
```

8.1.2 Operators for Complex Numbers
Addition is simply carried out as follows

```
: X+                 ( re1 im1 re2 im2 ... re1+re2 im1+im2 )
    ROT              ( re1 re2 im2 im1 ... )
    +                ( re1 re2 im1+im2 ... )
    >R               ( re1 re2 ... )
    +                ( re1+re2 ... )
    R>               ( re1+re2 im1+im2 ... )
; <Return> OK
```

Subtraction is

```
: X-                 ( re1 im1 re2 im2 ... re1-re2 im1-im2 )
    ROT              ( re1 re2 im2 im1 ... )
    SWAP             ( re1 re2 im1 im2 ... )
    -                ( re1 re2 im1-im2 ... )
    >R               ( re1 re2 ... )
    -                ( re1-re2 ... )
    R>               ( re1-re2 im1-im2 ... )
; <Return> OK
```

Multiplication by a real number is

```
: X*'                ( re im sc ... re*sc im*sc )
     SWAP OVER       ( re sc im sc ... )
     * ROT ROT *     ( im*sc re*sc ... )
     SWAP            ( re*sc im*sc ... )
; <Return> OK
```

Finally, multiplication of two complex numbers is

```
: X*                 ( r1 i1 r2 i2 ... r1.r2-i1.i2 r1.i2+r2.i1 )
  2OVER 2OVER        ( C1 C2 C1 C2 ... )
     ROT *           ( C1 C2 r1 r2 i1.i2 ... )
     >R * R> -       ( C1 C2 r1.r2-i1.i2 ... )
     >R              ( r1 i1 r2 i2 ... )
     ROT ROT *       ( r1 i2 i1.r2 ... )
     >R * R> +       ( r1.i2+i1.r2 ... )
     R>              ( r1.i2+i1.r2 r1.r2-i1.i2 ... )
     SWAP
; <Return> OK
```

The conjugate of a complex number is

```
: BAR MINUS ; <Return> OK
```

We can only access the modulus or the argument if we have the square root function SQR.

```
: R2 2OVER BAR X* ; <Return> OK
: MODULUS R2 SQR ; <Return> OK
: ARG            ( re im ... sine(argument) cosine(argument))
```

```
        2DUP          ( re im re im ... )
        MODULUS       ( re im d ... )
        1 SWAP /      ( re im 1/d ... )
        X*'
    ; <Return> OK
```

8.2 THE GAME OF LIFE

The rules of this game were first put forward in an article by Martin Gardner in the *Scientific American* in 1970. The game was originated by John Conway of the University of Cambridge.

The aim is to obtain a population of objects within a universe that will be born, live, reproduce and die, according to a very simple set of rules.

The criteria for the choice of these social rules are as follows

1. There can be no initial form which can be simply shown to be subject to unrestricted growth.
2. There must be initial forms that lead to unrestricted growth.
3. There must be initial forms which change over a very long period of time before finishing in one of the following three ways

    complete disappearance
    a stable form
    oscillating over two or more periods.

In short, the evolution of the population must not be predictable.

The environment of each cell is made up of the 8 cells adjacent to it (4 perpendicular and 4 diagonal).

The laws are as follows

Each cell with 2 or 3 neighbours survives.
Each cell having at least 4 neighbours dies of overpopulation, and each cell having less than 2 neighbours dies of isolation.
Each free space having 3 neighbours gives birth to a new cell.
Births and deaths take place simultaneously, and together represent a new generation.

Method

For obvious reasons, we shall restrict the field for the evolution of our 'society' to a fixed area of finite size.

The natural way to represent our 'universe' is by a grid in which the value of each cell indicates the presence or absence of an inhabitant. We shall use stars to indicate inhabited cells, with blank spaces everywhere else.

The problem is to prevent the births and deaths of the same generation from interfering in the algorithm. Therefore, the complete contents of the grid must be cleared, the cells subject to change located, the changes made - all simultaneously, so that the next generation can be produced.

The first idea that comes to mind is to use two grids. Although simple, this idea uses up a considerable amount of memory.

A more elegant solution is to code in each cell of the same memory not only the presence or absence of an element of generation N, but also data about its future in generation N+1.

The coding is as follows

Generation N	Generation N+1
Existent:1	Dead:5
	Surviving: 1 or 3
Non-existent:0	Birth:2
	Unchanged: 0 or 4

In other words, a cell will be occupied in generation N+1 if the value of this same cell on clearing generation N is 1, 2 or 3. In all other cases the cell will be empty.

We can already write the broad outlines of the algorithm, placing the number of stages on the stack before execution.

```
: GAME 0 DO
        DISPLAY        ( Displays generation N )
        GENERATE       ( Clears generation N )
        NORMALISE      ( Constructs generation N+1 )
     LOOP
     DISPLAY           ( Displays the most recent generation )
; <Return> OK
```

It now remains for us to define the words DISPLAY, GENERATE and NORMALISE, as well as the following

CLEAR which will reset the 'universe'
SET and RESET which will allow the population to be initialised.

The basic tool in the definition of all of these words is the definition word ARRAY which will allow the grid to be easily manipulated.

To define the universe grid, we write

```
DimensionX DimensionY ARRAY UNIVERSE
```

and to access a cell (X,Y) we type

```
X Y UNIVERSE
```

which will return to the stack the address of the corresponding cell.

The definition of ARRAY will be

```
: ARRAY              ( DimX DimY --- )
     <BUILDS
         OVER ,      ( Puts Dim> at Pfa+2 )
         * ALLOT     ( Reserves DimX * DimY bytes )
     DOES>
         DUP @       ( Places DimX on the stack )
         ROT *       ( Calculates IndY * DimX )
         +  +  2+    ( Calculates the absolute address of the cell )
; <Return> OK
```

Note that the indices of the grids generated by ARRAY evolve in the interval 0,DimX-1 * 0,DimY-1

The following words are now easily defined

```
: SET                          ( IndX IndY --- )
    UNIVERSE  1 SWAP  C!
;
: RESET                        ( IndX IndY --- )
    UNIVERSE  0 SWAP  C!
```

```
;
: CLEAR                         ( --- )
   DIMX  0  DO
       DIMY  0  DO
           I  J  RESET
       LOOP
   LOOP
; <Return> OK
```

DIMX and DIMY are two predefined constants that give the dimensions of the grid.

For the display, we write

```
: DISPLAY                             ( --- )
    HOMEUP                            ( Clears the screen )
    DIMY  0  DO
        DIMX  0  DO
            I  J  UNIVERSE  C @
            IF
                 ." *"
            ELSE
                SPACE
            THEN
        LOOP
        CR
    LOOP
; <Return> OK
```

Note that you will probably have to define HOMEUP for your own version of FORTH. In most cases you should be able to use

```
: HOMEUP  12  EMIT ; <Return> OK
```

The normalisation algorithm that takes into account the chosen code is very simple

```
: NORMALISE
   DIMY  0  DO
       DIMX  0  DO
           I  J  UNIVERSE DUP C@ ( Add val --- )
           DUP 3 >
           IF
              DROP  0            ( Add 0 --- )
           ELSE
              DUP  1 >
              IF
                 DROP  1         ( Add 1 --- )
              THEN
           THEN
           SWAP  C!              ( Store new value )
       LOOP
   LOOP
; <Return> OK
```

The word GENERATE forms the heart of the algorithm. It can be divided up into several functional blocks.

1. Clear all the elements in the grid.
2. In the case of each element, isolate the 3*3 sub-grid that surrounds it, taking into account any contact with the bounds of the grid.
3. Total all elements present in this sub-grid in generation N whose value is 1, 3 or 5; that is, those whose least significant bit is set.
4. Take away 1 if the element under examination exists in generation N.
5. As a consequence encode the value of the element in question.

```
: GENERATE                                  ( --- )
    DIMY  0  DO
        DIMX  0  DO
            0                               ( Neighbours counter )
            J  2+  DIMY  MIN
            J  1 - 0 MAX
            DO
                J  2+  DIMX  MIN
                J  1  -  0 MAX
                DO
                    I  J  UNIVERSE C@
                    1  AND  +
                LOOP
            LOOP
            I  J  UNIVERSE  C@
            1  AND                          ( Number of neighbours
                                              present --- )
            SWAP  OVER  -
            VERIFY                          ( Encode future )
            I  J  UNIVERSE  C!
        LOOP
    LOOP
; <Return> OK
```

A boolean value shows whether or not the element examined is inhabited in generation N. It determines the future of the cell under examination.

VERIFY comprises all the encoding of the element as a function of the number of neighbours and of the filled or empty state of the cell in generation N.

```
: VERIFY                  ( State number of neighbours --- )
    DUP  3  =             ( State number of neighbours b --- )
    IF
        DROP  2+          ( State+2 --- )
    ELSE
        2  =  0=          ( State State # 2 --- )
        IF
            4  +
        THEN
    THEN
; <Return> OK
```

The above definition gives the following table

N	N + 1			
	V=0 V=1	V=2	V=3	V>3
State=1 Occupied	State=State+4=5 (death through isolation)	Unchanged	State=State+2=3 (survives)	State=State+4=5
State=0 Empty	State=State+4=4 (unchanged)	Unchanged	State=State+2=2 (birth)	State=State+4=4 (unchanged)

8.3 TRIGONOMETRIC FUNCTIONS

The problem is to construct the classic trigonometric fixed-point functions, sine and cosine.

Since these functions are continuous, bounded and periodic, it is very easy to generate a table of their values.

The step is decided in advance, according to the precision required, that is, the position of the point. Here we have taken it to be to 4 figures.

The definitions are then immediate

```
: TABLE
     <BUILDS
      0 DO , LOOP
      DOES>
      SWAP 2 * + @
; <Return> OK
```

The word TABLE creates and fills a table whose number of entries is given as a parameter.

Here, SINTABLE contains 91 values of sine between 0° and 90°.

In order to be able to access this table for all possible angles, some precautions are necessary

```
: S180
      DUP 90 >
      IF
         180 SWAP -
      THEN
      SINTABLE
; <Return> OK
```

We then have

```
: SIN                          ( arg ... sine(arg) )
       360 MOD
       DUP 0<
       IF 360 + THEN
       DUP 180>
       IF 180 - S180 MINUS ELSE S180 THEN
; <Return> OK
: COS 90 + SIN ; <Return> OK
```

We can now write some tools using trigonometric functions

```
: ERRMATH ." VALUE TOO LARGE" QUIT ; <Return> OK
: TAN                        ( arg ... tangent(arg) )
      DUP SIN
      SWAP COS
      DUP ABS 2920 >
      IF 10000 SWAP */ ELSE DROP DROP ERRMATH THEN
; <Return> OK
```

8.4 THE TOWERS OF HANOI

This is a light-hearted but interesting problem. The priests of an oriental sect have to solve the following

> 64 disks are placed one upon the other on a spindle A, the diameters of the disks being of ever-decreasing size. The problem is to transfer all of these disks to another spindle C, using an intermediate spindle B.
>
> The only moves allowed are those where a disk is taken from the top of one stack and placed either upon a larger disk or on an empty spindle.

According to legend, the end of the world will occur when the priests solve the problem. To help them, we shall write a program to perform the required transfers of the disks.

We therefore have to construct an algorithm describing all the stages of transfer. In fact, this exercise is an example of an important class of recursive algorithms, for if we try an approach that always brings us back to the preceding problem, we can write

```
Shifting 64 disks from A to C is
Shift 63 disks from A to B
PRINT A to C
Shift 63 disks from B to C
```

The problem is increasingly simplified until there are no disks on one of the spindles, whereupon the problem 'shift 0 disk' is immediately solved.

We can therefore write a complete definition of 'Shift'.

```
Shift N disks from DEPARTURE to ARRIVAL
IF N#O THEN
   Shift N-1 disks from DEPARTURE to INTERMEDIARY
   PRINT DEPARTURE "TOWARDS" ARRIVAL
   Shift N-1 disks from INTERMEDIARY towards ARRIVAL
```

To set proper parameters, we number the spindles 1, 2 and 3. At any time, we have the relation

DEPARTURE + INTERMEDIARY + ARRIVAL = 6

and we can therefore write in FORTH

```
: HANOI                  ( d a n ... )
      SMUDGE
      DUP
      IF                 ( d a n ... )
```

```
            PREPARE-GO      ( d a n  d i n-1 ... )
            HANOI           ( d a n ... )
            EDIT
            PREPARE-RETURN  ( d a n i a  n-1 ... )²
            HANOI           ( d a n ... )
          THEN
          DROP DROP DROP
   SMUDGE
   ; <Return> OK
```

The words PREPARE prepare the stack for the following call

```
   : EDIT
        3DUP DROP SWAP CR . ." TOWARDS " .
   ; <Return> OK
   : PREPARE-GO                ( d a n ... d a n d i n-1 )
          3DUP                 ( d a n d a n ... )
          ROT ROT OVER +       ( d a n n d a d ... )
          6 SWAP - ROT 1 -     ( d a n d i n-1 ... )
   ; <Return> OK
   : PREPARE-RETURN                 ( d a n ... d a n i a n-1 )
          3DUP                      ( d a n d a n ... )
          SWAP ROT OVER +           ( d a n n a d a ... )
          6 SWAP - SWAP ROT 1 -     ( d a n i a  n-1 ... )
   ; <Return> OK
   : 3DUP ( n1 n2 n3 ... n1 n2 n3 n1 n2 n3 )
        DUP >R ROT
        DUP >R ROT
        DUP >R ROT
        R> R> SWAP R>
   ; <Return> OK
```

8.5 THE EIGHT QUEENS

This is another light-hearted problem, but less immediate than the previous one. The aim is to construct a word that will display on your screen a chessboard with eight queens positioned on it such that none can be taken by another.

If you try to do this physically, you will be tempted to think in terms of rows and columns, shifting the pieces row by row.

The solution can be formalised as follows

To place N queens on the board (8-N are already positioned)
Find the first row available for a queen
Find the first column available for a queen
Place the queen on this square
Place N-1 queens on the board

Note that we also have to allow for the trivial case of there being no more queens to place.

```
      THE EIGHT QUEENS

   0 VARIABLE SOLUTION       ( Contains the solution number )
   : VECTOR  <BUILDS HERE OVER ERASE ALLOT
             DOES> +         ( Returns the address of cell No. i )
   ; <Return> OK
```

```
1024 VECTOR COORDINATE
(Contents of COORDINATE ( No. of queens to be positioned + 1 )
     (Column of queen index i) times number of queens )
( The unpositioned queens will have column value 0 )
( The remainder will verify 0< column < number of queens + 1 )

: NBQ ( --- No. of queens + 1 ) 0 COORDINATE C@ ;
: SET ( row column --- )        SWAP COORDINATE C! ; ( positions
                                  a queen )
: RESET ( row --- )             0 SET ; ( withdraws a queen )
: FREE ( row n --- row flag )    (flag = 1 the queen is not in
                                  check)
                                 (flag = 0 the queen is in check)
     2DUP = >R
     OVER COORDINATE C@ OVER COORDINATE C@ -
     ROT ROT - ABS
     OVER ABS =
     SWAP 0=
     OR 0=
     R> OR
; <Return> OK
```

(FREE tests to see if the queen in row "row" is in check with queen "n" located in row "n".
It will be verified that the queen is not in check if

```
   ( row = n ) OR
NOT ( (column row) = column(n)) OR (|row - n| = column(row)
  - column(n) |) )
```

```
: ALL-FREE ( row --- row flag )   (flag = 1  the queen in row
                                             "row" is not in check
                                             with all queens so
                                             far positioned
                                   flag = 0  the queen is in check)
     1 OVER 1 DO
            OVER I FREE AND
     LOOP
; <Return> OK

: END-ROW ( row --- row flag )   (flag = 1  the queen in row "row"
    NBQ OVER COORDINATE C@ >                is on the board
; <Return> OK                     flag = 0  the queen in row "row"
                                            has moved beyond board
                                            to the right)
: DISPLAY ( --- )    (Displays the result)
        CR
        NBQ 1 DO
             I COORDINATE C@
             NBQ 1 DO
                   DUP I=
                   IF ." X" ELSE ." . " THEN
             LOOP
             DROP CR
        LOOP 1 SOLUTION +!
        CR ." Solution No. "  SOLUTION @ 3 .R
; <Return> OK
```

```
: INIT  ( --- )         (Initialises the board, with all queens in
                         column 0)
     NBQ 1 DO
         I RESET
     LOOP
     0 SOLUTION !
; <Return> OK


: FORWARD  ( row --- row flag )  (flag = 1 the queen in row "row"
   DUP DUP                        can be moved to the next column)
   COORDINATE C@ 1+ SET          (flag = 0 the queen cannot move
   END-ROW                        forward and is withdrawn from
                                  the board)
   IF 1 ELSE DUP RESET 0 THEN
; <Return> OK

: FIRST-FREE  ( row---row flag ) (flag = 1 the queen moves to the
    BEGIN                         first free column in its row)
       FORWARD                   (flag = 0 move impossible)
       IF ALL-FREE -DUP
       ELSE 0 1 THEN
    UNTIL
; <Return> OK

: POSITION  ( row --- flag )  [ SMUDGE ]
      NBQ OVER > IF
         BEGIN  FIRST-FREE
                IF 1+ POSITION  -DUP
                ELSE 1- 0 1 THEN
         UNTIL
      ELSE DISPLAY 1- 0  THEN
[ SMUDGE ]
; <Return> OK

: QUEENS     ( Number of queens --- )
     1 +  0 SWAP SET
     INIT
     1 POSITION
     2DROP
; <Return> OK
```

In order to solve the eight queens problem, we simply type

```
8 QUEENS <Return>
```

and the result is displayed.

8.6 PERPETUAL GREGORIAN CALENDAR

The problem here is to find on what day of the week any given date falls.

A detailed analysis of the problem has shown that, starting from the year 1582, the following three formulas are valid.

For the months of January to February

```
Factor =  365 * Year
         +Day
         +31 * ( Month-1 )
         -INT( 3/4(INT(Year/100) + 1) )
         +INT( (Year-1)/4 )
```

For the months March to December

```
Factor =  365 * Year
         +Day
         +31 * ( Month-1 )
         -INT( 3/4(INT(Year/100) + 1) )
         -INT( 0.4 * Month + 2.3 )
         +INT( Year/4 )
```

The final formula is then

```
No. day of the week = Factor MOD 7  (Taking Saturday to be day
                                     No. 0)
```

Note that there is only a small part where the two formulas differ; hence the following two words

```
: JANUARY/FEBRUARY   ( Year Month ---n )
     DROP 1 -        ( Year-1 --- )
     4 /             ( INT((Year-1)/4) --- )
; <Return> OK

: MARCH/DECEMBER     ( Year Month ---n )
     4 * 23 + 10 /   ( Year INT(0.4*Month+2.3) --- )
     SWAP 4 /        ( INT(0.4*Month+2.3) INT(Year/4) --- )
     SWAP -
; <Return> OK
```

Here is a word that displays the day of the week as a function of its number.

```
: DISPLAY
     DUP 0=
     IF ." SATURDAY"
     ELSE
        DUP 1 =
        IF ." SATURDAY"
        ELSE
           DUP 2 =
           IF ." MONDAY"
           ELSE
              DUP 3 =
              IF ." TUESDAY"
              ELSE
```

```
                    DUP 4 =
                    IF ." WEDNESDAY"
                    ELSE
                       DUP 5 =
                       IF ." THURSDAY"
                       ELSE
                          DUP 6 =
                          IF ." FRIDAY"
        THEN THEN THEN THEN THEN THEN THEN
        DROP
        CR
    ; <Return> OK
```

Since some results are in double length, we shall use in the definition words that follow mixed operators.

First we must define a word that leaves the modulus of a double-length number

```
    : DMOD          ( D n ... mod )
        M/MOD  DROP  DROP
    ; <Return> OK
```

The date will be accessible on the data stack from the following

```
                                  ( Day Month Year --- )
    : DAY                         ( D M Y --- )
        DUP 365 M*                ( D M Y d --- )
        >R >R  ROT                ( M Y D --- )
        0  R> R> D+               ( M Y d --- )
        2SWAP  2DUP  >R >R        ( d M Y --- )
        100 / 1+ 3 4 */           ( d M n --- )
        SWAP 1 - 31 *             ( d n n' --- )
        SWAP - 0 D+               ( d --- )
        R>  R>                    ( d M Y --- )
        SWAP DUP 3<               ( d Y M flag --- )
        IF
           JANUARY/FEBRUARY
        ELSE
           MARCH/DECEMBER
        THEN                      ( d n --- )
        0 D+                      ( Factor --- )
        7 DMOD                    ( No. D --- )
        DISPLAY                   ( --- )
    ; <Return> OK
```

You can now type, for example

```
    7 12 1982 DAY <Return> TUESDAY
    OK
```

8.7 FILE CREATION AND MANAGEMENT

The aim of this problem is to be able to create and use a file. The data we shall use will take the following form: Surname, First name, Telephone, Company.

Each of these groups will be called a record, and each class of information within a record will be called a field.

We shall provide the three words that will permit the basic manipulation of the data; that is, write, modify and read. As we shall see, other words can easily be written.

We shall use the mass storage facility that FORTH provides, chiefly the word BLOCK.

Let us begin by defining four constants that will give the characteristics of the file

RL is the length of a record. Here 64 characters.

FB is the number of the first block of mass storage to be used for the file.

BR is the number of records contained in a block; that is, the number of bytes per block divided by the length of a record (RL).

MR is the maximum number of records in the file - a multiple of BR.

The blocks that make up the file are those that sequentially follow FB. Thus, FB must be very carefully chosen so that there are sufficient free blocks after it.

We shall also need five other variables.

REC which will be the record pointer; that is, the number of the record to be processed.

SRCH which will contain the address of a look-up table for a search.

SRCH1 used for a vectored execution.

SRCH2 also used for a vectored execution.

STRT which will be the record number from where a search will start.

We shall also need four two-element tables, each corresponding to a field and containing the field length, together with its position in the record (tabulation). To achieve this we need the following definition word

```
: DEF
     <BUILDS , ,
     DOES>
; <Return> OK
```

The tables will then be defined as follows

```
16 0 DEF SURNAME
12 16 DEF FIRST-NAME
13 28 DEF TELEPHONE
23 41 DEF COMPANY
```

In a record the maximum number of characters for the surname is 16, for the first name 12, for the telephone 13 and for the company name 23.

First we write a word START which resets the record number and a word NEXT which increments it by one.

```
: START
     0 REC !
; <Return> OK
: NEXT
     1 REC +!
; <Return> OK
```

We shall now write a word REC->ADDR which, beginning with the contents of REC, will calculate in which block this record is located, load it into memory if it is not there already, and leave on the stack the memory address that marks the start of this record.

```
: REC->ADDR               ( --- Addr )
        REC @ BR /MOD     ( Incr No block --- )
        FB  + BLOCK       ( Incr Addr --- )
        SWAP RL * +       ( Addr --- )
; <Return> OK
```

The next step is to write a word which, with the table address of one of the fields (SURNAME, FIRST-NAME, TELEPHONE, COMPANY) on the stack, leaves on the stack the address of this field in the record pointed to (by REC), as well as the number of characters that go to make it up (16,12,13,23).

```
: ?FIELD                        ( Field --- Addr Length )
     DUP @ SWAP  2+ @ SWAP      ( Length Tab --- )
     REC->ADDR                  ( Length Tab Addr --- )
     +  SWAP                    ( Addr Length --- )
; <Return> OK
```

It is now very simple to write a word .FIELD which, with the field address on the stack, will display the contents of the record field pointed to by REC.

```
: .FIELD         ( Field --- )
     ?FIELD      ( Addr Length --- )
     TYPE
; <Return> OK
```

Similarly, it is equally easy to write the word FIELD! which, again with the field address on the stack, will record any typed text in the chosen record field pointed to by REC.

```
: FIELD!                     ( Field --- )
       44 TEXT PAD SWAP      ( Addr Pad Field --- )
       ?FIELD CMOVE UPDATE
; <Return> OK
```

The reader will note that 44 is the ASCII code for comma, which we have chosen to be the separator.

In order to be able to write easily into the file, we need to have a word that finds the first free record. Such a record will be identified by having a blank space as its first character.

Similarly, we shall need a word that is capable of finding the record whose specified field contains a particular item of data provided by the user.

Both of these words contain a common part; they differ only in the type of comparison that each makes. We shall therefore use vectored execution with the word SEARCH.

```
: SEARCH                                     ( --- )
       1 MR STRT  @ DO                       ( 1 --- )
                        I REC !
                        SRCH1 @ EXECUTE      ( 1 Flag --- )
                        IF 0= LEAVE THEN     ( 1 --- )
```

```
        LOOP
        IF SRCH2 @ EXECUTE THEN
    ; <Return> OK
```

We now write the word FREE which finds the first empty record and places its number in REC.

```
    : FREE1                        ( ---Flag )
          REC->ADDR C@ 32 =        ( Flag --- )
    ; <Return> OK
    : FULL                         ( --- )
         ." FILE FULL"
    ; <Return> OK
    : FREE
         ' FREE1 CFA SRCH1 !       ( --- )
         ' FULL CFA SRCH2 !
         0 STRT ! SEARCH
    ; <Return> OK
```

Note that here the search for a empty record begins at number 0 (0 STRT !). It is also perfectly possible to create another word that will avoid having to plough through the complete file every time. There are a number of algorithms available that do this. For smaller files the word we have defined above has the advantage of using deleted records.

The word FIND, which finds a record whose specified field corresponds to the required text, is written

```
    : FIND1                        ( --- Flag )
          PAD SRCH @ ?FIELD        ( Addr Length --- )
          SWAP -TEXT 0=            ( Flag --- )
    ; <Return> OK
    : MISSING                      ( --- )
           ." NONEXISTENT"
    ; <Return> OK
    : FIND                         ( --- )
        [COMPILE] '  2+ SRCH !
        ' FIND1 CFA SRCH1 !
        ' MISSING CFA SRCH2 !
        0  STRT  ! 44 TEXT
        SEARCH
    ; <Return> OK
```

The word FIND is used in the following way

FIND FIELD XXXXXXXXXXXXX

where FIELD is SURNAME or FIRST-NAME or TELEPHONE or COMPANY and XXXXXXXXXXXXX is the required text.

If your FORTH does not have the words TEXT and -TEXT, here they are defined

```
   : TEXT PAD 72 32 FILL WORD HERE COUNT PAD SWAP CMOVE ;
   : -TEXT 2DUP + SWAP DO DROP 2+ DUP 2 - @ I @ - DUP IF DUP
   ABS / LEAVE THEN 2 +LOOP SWAP DROP ;
```

We can now define the words to be used by the user.

```
: WRITE
        FREE
        SURNAME FIELD!
        FIRST-NAME FIELD!
        TELEPHONE FIELD!
        COMPANY FIELD!
        FLUSH
; <Return> OK
```

For example, to make a record of Smith John 9999999 Forth, we must type

```
WRITE SMITH,JOHN,9999999,FORTH <Return> OK
: DISPLAY
       SURNAME .FIELD
       FIRST-NAME .FIELD
       TELEPHONE .FIELD
       COMPANY .FIELD
; <Return> OK
```

The above allows the contents of the record pointed to by REC to be displayed.

```
: LOOK
      FIND DISPLAY
; <Return> OK
```

This word is used in the same way as FIND.

```
: OTHER
       NEXT REC @ STRT !
       SEARCH DISPLAY
; <Return> OK
```

After a first search has been carried out using the word FIND, the use of OTHER enables us to see if there is another record in the file that agrees with what we are seeking. This word can be used repeatedly until the entire file has been searched. We can of course write a word that will examine the file for all matches, whatever their number, using LOOK and OTHER in the loop structure BEGIN...WHILE... REPEAT.

```
: CHANGE
        [COMPILE]
        FIELD!
; <Return> OK
```

Once we have located the correct record, using the above word we can alter the contents of one of the fields in the following way

```
CHANGE FIELD XXXXXX <Return> OK
```

where FIELD is SURNAME or FIRST-NAME or TELEPHONE or COMPANY and XXXXXX is the new text.

```
: DELETE
        REC->ADDR RL 32 FILL
        UPDATE FLUSH
; <Return> OK
```

When a record is located, we can use this word to delete it by typing

```
DELETE <Return> OK
```

Of course, the values of the different constants chosen for this example can be altered. Those that we have chosen have the advantage of providing a listing in blocks that can be quickly obtained by simply typing LIST.

Other user words can be defined from those given, depending on the required application.

Appendix 1: The FORTH, Inc. Line * Editor (S. H. Daniel)

THE EDITOR COMMANDS
The word 'text' following a command indicates that any text typed after the command will be copied to the text buffer used by that command. The buffer contents will then be used when the command executes. If no text is typed by the user, the contents of that buffer (left over from the previous command or commands) will be used without modification in the execution of the command.

X   eXtract   (--)

Copies the current line into the INSERT buffer, and removes it from the screen. All following lines are moved up, and line 15 is left blank.

T   Type   (n --)

Type line n from the current screen. Set the cursor to the start of the line.

L   List   (--)

Like the FORTH word LIST, except that the current screen number is obtained from the variable SCR, rather than being typed in by the user.

N   Next   (--)

Increments the current screen number by one. This command is used just before the L command, to allow the user to list the next sequential screen.

B   Back   (--)

Decrements the current screen number by one. This command is also used before the L command, to allow listing of the previous sequential screen.

P   Put   (--)
P text

---

* Reprinted from *Forth Dimensions*, a publication of the Forth Interest Group (P.O. Box 1105, San Carlos, California 94070. $15.00 U.S. or $27.00 overseas airmail per year).

Any following text will be copied into the INSERT buffer. The INSERT buffer will be copied into the current line, replacing its previous contents. If the text consists of one or more blanks, the current line will be erased.

WIPE   Wipe   (--)

Erases the current screen. Equivalent to the original CLEAR command, except that the user need not enter the screen number.

COPY Copy   (from -2, to-1 --)

Copy one screen to another.

F   Find   (--)
F text

Any following text is copied to the INSERT buffer. The contents of the INSERT buffer are compared to the contents of the current line. If a match is found, the line is displayed with the cursor positioned immediately after the end of the string searched for. The F command, with no following text, is exactly the same as the previous editor command N. If no match is found, the requested string is echoed to the terminal and the error message "NONE" is output.

E   Erase   (--)

Erases backwards from the cursor, according to the number of characters in the FIND buffer. This command should only be used immediately after the F command.

D   Delete   (--)
D text

Any following text is copied into the FIND buffer. The D command is a combination of the F and E commands. The string in the FIND buffer is matched against the contents of the current line, and if a match is found, the found string is deleted from the line.

TILL   Till   (--)
TILL text

Any following text is copied into the FIND buffer. Starting from the current cursor position, TILL searches for a match with the contents of the FIND buffer. If a match is found, TILL deletes all the text on the line from the current cursor position up to any including the end of the matched text.

S   Search   (last screen#+1 --)
S text

Any following text is copied into the FIND buffer. Starting at the top of the current screen and continuing until the bottom of the screen immediately before the screen number on the top of the stack, S searches for a match to the contents of the FIND buffer. Whenever a match is found, the line containing the match will be typed out, along with the line number and screen number in which the match occurred. Because of the way FORTH handles loops, the number on the top of the stack must be one higher than the highest screen to be searched.

```
I     Insert   ( -- )
I text
```

Any following text will be copied into the INSERT buffer. The I command copies the contents of the INSERT buffer into the current line, starting at the current cursor position. Any text to the right of the cursor will be pushed to the right and will be pushed off the line and lost if the total length of the line exceeds 64 characters.

```
U     Under   ( -- )
U text
```

Any following text will be copied into the INSERT buffer. Spread the screen at the line immediately below the current line, leaving a blank line. All following lines are pushed down. Any text on line 15 will be lost. The contents of the INSERT buffer will be copied into the blank line, and that line will be made the current line.

```
R     Replace   ( -- )
R text
```

Any following text is copied into the INSERT buffer. The R command operates as a combination of the E (Erase) and I (Insert) commands. Starting at the current cursor position, and working backwards towards the start of the line, text corresponding to the length of the contents of the FIND buffer is deleted, and the contents of the INSERT buffer are inserted into the line. Since the contents of the FIND buffer determine how much text will be erased, the R command should only be used immediately following the F (Find) command.

```
M   Move   ( Block#, Line# -- )
```

Copies the current line into the INSERT buffer, then copies the INSERT buffer to the block, specified by Block#, UNDER the line specified by LINE#. The original block number is restored, and the next line in the block becomes the current line. This allows sequential lines to be moved with a minimum of keystrokes. One unfortunate side-effect of this command is that to move something to line 0 of another screen, you must first move it UNDER line 0, using the command xxx 0 M, make screen xxx current, and then extract the old line 0, moving everything else up.

```
↑        ( -- )
```

Used as a terminator for all commands allowing text input, such as P, F, R, etc. Allows more than one command to be entered on a single line, e.g.,

```
3 T P  This is line 3↑ L (cr)
```

Although useful, this feature does preclude the use of the " " as a character in any text to be put on a screen.

GLOSSARY

The following glossary addresses all the FORTH words in the line editor except the actual editing commands, which are discussed above.

TEXT (delimiter --)

Any following text in the input stream, up to but not including the delimiter, is moved to the PAD. The length of the input string is stored at PAD, with the actual string starting at PAD+1. In FORTH-79 Standard systems, if no text follows in the input stream, a length byte of 0 will be stored. In non-Standard systems, a length byte of 1 will be stored, but PAD+1 will contain a null to indicate the absence of text.

(LINE) (Line#, Screen# -- Buffer Address,64)

Using the line and screen numbers, computes the starting memory address of the line in the disk buffer. May not be necessary in FORTH-79 Standard systems, depending upon implementation. Should already be present in earlier implementations.

LINE (Line# -- Buffer Address)

Ensures that the line number is within the legal range of the current screen, then uses (LINE) to set the starting address of the line in the disk buffer.

WHERE (Offset,Block# --)

Used when a compile time error occurs during loading. Converts the block number to a screen number, makes that screen current, and prints the line in which the load error occurred. Underneath the line in error, the cursor is printed to show the approximate location of the error. Enables the EDITOR vocabulary as it exists. Strictly speaking, this is not part of the polyFORTH editor, but it is a highly useful tool.

#LOCATE (-- Cursor offset,line#)

Uses the current cursor position to compute the line number which contains the cursor and the offset from the beginning of the line to the current cursor position.

#LEAD (--Line address,offset to cursor)

Computes the beginning address of the current line in the disk buffer and the offset from the start of the line to the current cursor position.

#LAG (-- cursor address, count after cursor)

Computes the address of the cursor in the disk buffer and the count of characters remaining on the line after the cursor.

-MOVE (from address, to line# --)

Moves a line within the disk buffer to the line specified, completely replacing the previous contents of that line.

?MOVE (destination buffer address --)

If any text has been entered into the PAD by TEXT, moves that text to the specified buffer. Used to load the FIND and INSERT buffers for searches, etc. If no text was in the PAD, no action is taken.

>LINE# (-- current line number)

Uses the stored cursor location to compute the current line number.

FIND-BUF (--)

Establishes the FIND buffer a fixed distance above the current address of the PAD.

INSERT-BUF (--)

Establishes the INSERT buffer a fixed distance above the FIND buffer.

(HOLD) (Line# --)

Non-destructively copies the contents of the current line to the INSERT buffer.

(KILL) (Line# --)

Replaces the specified line with a blank line.

(SPREAD) (--)

Spreads the screen, starting at the current line, pushing all lines below the current line down, and leaving the current line blank. Any text on line 15 is pushed off the screen and is lost.

DISPLAY-CURSOR (--)

Displays the current line with the cursor in place.

(R) (--)

Replaces the current line with the contents of the INSERT buffer. Used as the primitive operation for the P command.

(TOP) (--)

Resets the stored cursor position to the top of the screen.

1LINE (-- Flag)

Scans the current line for an exact match with the contents of the FIND buffer. If a match is found, the stored cursor position is updated.

(SEEK) (--)

Starting at the current cursor position, searches the rest of the current screen for an exact match to the contents of the FIND buffer. If no match is found, the contents of the FIND buffer are typed and the error message "NONE" is output.

DELETE (Count --)

Starting at the current cursor position, text is deleted backwards (towards the beginning of the line), according to the count. The remaining text on the line is moved to the left and the end of the line is filled with blanks.

(F) (--)

Copies any following text to the FIND buffer and searches the current screen for a match. Used as the primitive operation for the F and D commands.

(E) (--)

Uses the length of the contents of the FIND buffer to set the count for (DELETE). Used as the primitive for the E and R commands.

COUNTER

A variable used by the S command to count the number of lines output to the screen and printer.

BUMP (--)

Increments the number of lines output and sends a page eject when 56 lines have been output. Used by the S command to handle pagination on the console and printer.

ERROR MESSAGES

Only two error messages are output by the line editor:

NONE

Indicates that no match was found on the current screen corresponding to the contents of the FIND buffer.

NOT ON CURRENT EDITING SCREEN

Indicates that the line number passed to the word LINE was outside the legal range of 0-15 decimal.

```
SCR # 200
( fol9FORTH compatible line editor                    310715 SHD )
FORTH  DEFINITIONS  HEX
: TEXT                 ( accept following text to PAD )
    HERE  C/L  1+  BLANKS  WORD
    HERE  PAD  C/L  1+  CMOVE  ;
: LINE                  ( relative to SCR, leave address of line )
    DUP  0FFF0  AND
    IF  ." NOT ON CURRENT EDITING SCREEN"  QUIT  THEN
    SCR  @  (LINE)  DROP  ;
-->
```

```
SCR # 201
( WHERE, #LOCATE                                      810707 SHD )
VOCABULARY  EDITOR  IMMEDIATE  HEX
: WHERE               ( print screen # and image of error )
   DUP  B/SCR  /  DUP  SCR  !  ." SCR # "  DECIMAL  .
   SWAP  C/L  /MOD  C/L  *  ROT  BLOCK  +  CR  C/L  TYPE
   CR  HERE  C@  -  SPACES  5E  EMIT
   [COMPILE]  EDITOR  QUIT  ;
EDITOR  DEFINITIONS
: #LOCATE             (  --- cursor offset-2, line-1 )
   R#  @  C/L  /MOD  ;
-->

SCR # 202
( #LEAD, #LAG, -MOVE, BUF-MOVE                        810707 SHD )
: #LEAD               (  --- line address-2, offset to cursor-1)
   #LOCATE  LINE  SWAP  ;
: #LAG                (  --- cursor adr-2, count after cursor-1)
   #LEAD  DUP  >R  +  C/L R>  -  ;
: -MOVE               ( move from adr-2, to line-1 ---  )
   LINE  C/L  CMOVE  UPDATE  ;
: BUF-MOVE            ( move text to buffer-1, if any  --- )
   PAD  1+  C@
   IF  PAD  SWAP  C/L  1+  CMOVE
   ELSE  DROP
   THEN  ;              -->

SCR # 203
( >LINE#, FIND-BUF, INSERT-BUF                        810707 SHD )
: >LINE#              ( convert current cursor position to line#)
   #LOCATE  SWAP  DROP  ;
: FIND-BUF            ( buffer used for all searches )
   PAD  50  +  ;
: INSERT-BUF          ( buffer used for all insertions )
   FIND-BUF  50  +  ;
-->

SCR # 204
( (HOLD-, (KILL-, (SPREAD-, X                         810707 SHD )
: (HOLD)              ( move line-1 from block to insert buffer )
   LINE  INSERT-BUF  1+  C/L  DUP  INSERT-BUF  C!  CMOVE  ;
: (KILL)              ( erase line-1 with blanks )
   LINE  C/L  BLANKS  UPDATE  ;
: (SPREAD)            ( spread, making line# blank )
   >LINE#  DUP  1  -  0E
   DO  I  LINE  I  1+  -MOVE  -1  +LOOP  (KILL)  ;
: X             ( delete line# from block, put in insert buffer)
   >LINE#  DUP  (HOLD)  0F  DUP  ROT
   DO  I  1+  LINE  I  -MOVE  LOOP  (KILL)  ;
-->
```

```
SCR # 205
( DISPLAY-CURSOR, T, L                              810715 SHD )
: DISPLAY-CURSOR    ( -- )
   CR  SPACE  #LEAD  TYPE  5E  EMIT
   #LAG  TYPE  #LOCATE  .  DROP  ;
: T                   ( type line#-1 )
   C/L  *  R#  !  0  DISPLAY-CURSOR  ;
: L                   ( list current screen )
   SCR  @  LIST  ;
-->
```

```
SCR # 206
( N, B, (TOP-, SEEK-ERROR                           810707 SHD )
: N                   ( select next sequential screen )
   1  SCR  +!  ;
: B                   ( select previous sequential screen )
   -1  SCR  +!  ;
: (TOP)               ( reset cursor to top of block )
   0  R#  !  ;
: SEEK-ERROR           ( output error msg if no match )
   (TOP)  FIND-BUF  HERE  C/L  1+  CMOVE
   HERE  COUNT  TYPE
   ." NONE"  QUIT  ;
-->
```

```
SCR # 207
( (R-, P                                            810707 SHD )
: (R)                 ( replace current line with insert buffer )
   >LINE#
   INSERT-BUF  1+  SWAP  -MOVE  ;
: P                   ( following text in insert buffer and line)
   5E  TEXT
   INSERT-BUF  BUF-MOVE
   (R)  ;
-->
```

```
SCR # 208
( WIPE, COPY, 1LINE                                 810715 SHD )
: WIPE                ( clear the current screen )
   10  0  DO  I  (KILL)  LOOP  ;
: COPY                ( copy screen-2 onto screen-1 )
   B/SCR  *  OFFSET  @  +  SWAP  B/SCR  *  B/SCR
   OVER  +  SWAP
   DO  DUP  FORTH  I  BLOCK  2  -  !  1+  UPDATE  LOOP
   DROP  FLUSH  ;
```

```
: 1LINE       ( scan current line for match with FIND buffer )
              ( update cursor, return boolean                )
   #LAG  FIND-BUF  COUNT  MATCH  R#  +!  ;
-->
```

```
SCR # 209
( (SEEK-, (DELETE-                                   810715 SHD )
: (SEEK)      ( FIND buffer match over full screen, else error)
   BEGIN  3FF  R#  @  <
     IF  SEEK-ERROR  THEN
     1LINE
   UNTIL  ;
: (DELETE)           ( backwards at cursor by count-1 )
   >R  #LAG  +  R  -          ( save blank fill location )
   #LAG  R  MINUS  R#  +!     ( back up cursor )
   #LEAD  +  SWAP  CMOVE
   R>  BLANKS  UPDATE  ;      ( fill from end of text )
 -->
```

```
SCR # 210
( (F-, F, (E-, E                                     810715 SHD )
: (F)                ( find occurance of following text )
   5E  TEXT
   FIND-BUF  BUF-MOVE
   (SEEK)  ;
: F                  ( find and display following text )
   (F)  DISPLAY-CURSOR  ;
: (E)                ( erase backwards from cursor )
   FIND-BUF  C@  (DELETE)  ;
: E                  ( erase and display line )
   (E)  DISPLAY-CURSOR  ;
-->
```

```
SCR # 211
( D, TILL                                            810715 SHD )
: D                  ( find, delete, and display following text)
   (F)  E  ;
: TILL               ( delete from cursor to text end )
   #LEAD  +  5E  TEXT
   FIND-BUF  BUF-MOVE
   1LINE  0=  IF  SEEK-ERROR  THEN
   #LEAD  +  SWAP  -  (DELETE)
   DISPLAY-CURSOR  ;
-->
```

```
SCR # 212
( COUNTER, BUMP                                          810707 SHD )
0  VARIABLE  COUNTER
: BUMP                ( the line number and handle paging )
   1  COUNTER  +!   COUNTER  @
   38 >  IF   0 COUNTER !
   CR  CR  0F  MESSAGE  0C  EMIT  THEN  ;
-->
```

```
SCR # 213
( S                                                      810715 SHD )
: S                   ( from current to screen-1 for string )
   0C  EMIT  5E  TEXT   0  COUNTER !
   FIND-BUF  BUF-MOVE
   SCR  @  DUP  >R  DO  I  SCR  !
   (TOP)
   BEGIN
      1LINE  IF  DISPLAY-CURSOR  SCR  ?  BUMP  THEN
      3FF  R#  @  <
   UNTIL
   LOOP  R>  SCR  !  ;
-->
```

```
SCR # 214
( I, U                                                   810715 SHD )
: I                   ( insert text within line )
   5E  TEXT                      ( load insert buffer with text)
   INSERT-BUF  BUF-MOVE          ( if any )
   INSERT-BUF  COUNT  #LAG  ROT  OVER  MIN  >R
   R  R#  +!                     ( bump cursor )
   R  -  >R                      ( characters to save )
   DUP  HERE  R  CMOVE           ( from old cursor to HERE )
   HERE  #LEAD  +  R>  CMOVE     ( HERE to cursor location )
   R>  CMOVE  UPDATE             ( PAD to old cursor )
   DISPLAY-CURSOR  ;             ( look at new line )
: U                   ( insert following text under current line)
   C/L  R#  +!  (SPREAD)  P  ;
-->
```

```
SCR # 215
( R, M                                                   810715 SHD )
: R                   ( replace found text with insert buffer )
   (E)  I  ;
: M                   ( move from current line on current screen )
   SCR  @  >R         ( to screen-2, UNDER line-1 )
```

```
     R#  @  >R          ( save original screen and cursor location )
     >LINE#  (HOLD)     ( move current line to insert buffer )
     SWAP  SCR  !       ( set new screen # )
     1+  C/L  *  R#  ! ( text is stored UNDER requested line )
     (SPREAD)  (R)      ( store insert buffer in new screen )
     R>  C/L  +  R#  ! ( set original cursor to next line )
     R>  SCR  !  ;      ( restore original screen )

FORTH  DEFINITIONS  DECIMAL
```

```
SCR # 216
(                                                  810715 SHD )
FORTH  DEFINITIONS  DECIMAL
: 2DROP   DROP  DROP  ;       ( drop a double number )

: 2SWAP                       ( 2nd double number to TOS )
    ROT  >R  ROT  R>  ;

: 2DUP    OVER  OVER  ;       ( dup a double number )

: (MATCH)                     ( addr-3, addr-2, count-1 -- flag )
    -DUP  IF  OVER  +  SWAP
              DO
                  DUP  C@  I  C@  -
                  IF  0=  LEAVE  ELSE  1+  THEN
              LOOP
          ELSE  DROP  0=  THEN  ;                         -->
```

```
SCR # 217
(                                                  810715 SHD )

: MATCH            ( cursor adr-4, bytes left-3, string adr-2 )
                   ( string count-1 -- flag-2, cursor offset-1 )
    >R  >R  2DUP  R>  R>  2SWAP  OVER  +  SWAP
    ( caddr-6, bleft-5, $addr-4, $len-3, caddr+bleft-2, caddr-1)
    DO
        2DUP  I  SWAP  (MATCH)
        IF
            >R  2DROP  R>  -  I  SWAP  -  0  SWAP  0  0  LEAVE
        ( caddr, bleft, $addr, $len    OR    0, offset, 0, 0 )
        THEN
    LOOP
    2DROP   ( caddr-2, bleft-1    OR    0-2, offset-1 )
    SWAP  0=  SWAP  ;
```

Appendix 2: An Alternative FORTH Editor

In chapter 4 we discussed the necessary editor commands and their functions. It is in fact a very good exercise to write an editor.

This appendix gives an example of an editor that you can use and improve.

The words are sufficiently simple not to require too many comments; this will enable you to get used to reading FORTH without comments.

The blocks are 1024 bytes in size (single screen), and each screen consists of 16 lines each containing 64 characters.

The blocks of text are stored either in the disk-buffers, or in the screen-buffer.

The screen number corresponds to the physical address of the block on the screen in the mass store. Its value is held in the user variable SCR.

The cursor position in the screen-buffer is held in another user variable R#.

The text that we want to insert into or remove from the screen buffer is held temporarily in the text buffer area, pointed to by the word PAD, which returns a memory address located 68 bytes above the dictionary pointer DP. PAD is used like a scratch pad while the current line is edited.

All the defined words are grouped in the EDITOR vocabulary, which is defined as follows

```
VOCABULARY EDITOR IMMEDIATE <Return> OK
```

To make the EDITOR vocabulary CURRENT, we then only need to type

```
EDITOR DEFINITIONS <Return> OK
```

All the following definitions will be added to EDITOR instead of being treated like ordinary FORTH definitions.

Two base words are used to carry out the line editing functions - TEXT and LINE.

TEXT moves a line of text from the input stream to the text buffer area of the PAD.

LINE calculates the address of the line in the screen buffer.

```
FORTH DEFINITIONS HEX
: TEXT          ( c --- c is the delimiter character )
    HERE        ( Start address of the word buffer into which the )
                ( text interpreter places the characters )
    C/L 1+      ( Number of characters per line + 1 )
    BLANKS      ( Makes blank )
```

```
     WORD          ( Moves the text, delimited by c, from the input )
     HERE          ( stream to the word buffer )
     PAD           ( Text buffer address )
     C/L 1+        ( Number of characters per line + 1 )
     CMOVE         ( Moves the text, 64 bytes + length, to PAD )
  ; <Return> OK

  : LINE         ( n --- addr returns the address of the beginning of )
                 ( line)
                 ( n in the screen buffer.  Loads the block if it is )
                 ( not )
                 ( yet in the disk-buffers. )
    DUP
    FF0  AND
    17  ?ERROR ( Ensures that it lies between 0 and 15 )
    SCR @        ( Displays the current screen number )
    (LINE)       ( Transfers the screen from the disk buffer to the )
                 ( screen buffer and possibly loads a block into the )
                 ( disk-buffers.  Calculates the address of the nth )
                 ( line of the screen buffer and places it on the )
                 ( stack. )
    DROP
  ; <Return> OK
```

The following words, in the EDITOR vocabulary, can then be put directly into use

```
  VOCABULARY EDITOR IMMEDIATE HEX
  EDITOR DEFINITIONS
  : -MOVE             ( Addr n --- copies a line of text starting at )
                      ( address Addr in the nth line of the current )
                      ( screen buffer )

      LINE            ( Calculates the address of line n )
      C/L  CMOVE      ( Moves 64 characters in the address to line n )
      UPDATE          ( Informs the disk handler that the block has been )
                      ( altered )
  ; Return> OK

  : H                 ( n --- copies the nth line of the screen buffer in )
                      ( PAD.  The text is then ready to be displayed )

    LINE              ( Calculates the line address )
    PAD 1+            ( Begin address of PAD )
    C/L DUP           ( Number of characters per line )
    PAD C!            ( Sets the length of PAD to 64 )
    CMOVE             ( Moves the nth line )
  ; <Return> OK

  : E                 ( n --- erases the nth line, filling it with 64 )
                      ( blanks )
    LINE              ( Line address )
    C/L BLANKS        ( Blanks )
    UPDATE            ( Buffer flag )
  ; <Return> OK
```

```
: S               ( n --- blanks the nth line and shifts towards the )
                  ( bottom the old line and all those that follow one )
                  ( by one.  The last line is lost )
   DUP 1-         ( Last line to be shifted )
   0EH            ( 14, the number of the last line to be shifted )
   DO
   I  LINE        ( Calculates the address of the nth line )
   I  1+          ( Next line number )
   -MOVE          ( Shift of a line to the bottom )
   -1  +LOOP      ( Decrements the loop counter by 1 )
   E              ( Erases the nth line )
; <Return> OK

: D               ( Deletes the nth line from the screen buffer and )
                  ( scrolls up all the remaining lines by 1.  The de-)
                  ( leted line remains in PAD )
   DUP H          ( Copies the nth line in PAD )
   0FH            ( Number of the last line )
   DUP ROT
   DO
   I 1+ LINE      ( Address of line to be shifted )
   I -MOVE        ( Shifts upwards by one )
   LOOP
   E              ( Erases the last line )
; <Return> OK

: R               ( n --- replaces the nth line by the text held in )
                  ( PAD )
   PAD 1+         ( Begin address of PAD )
   SWAP - MOVE    ( Copies the text from PAD in the nth line )
; <Return> OK

: P               ( n --- places the text that follows in the nth )
                  ( line.  The old text is lost )
   1  TEXT        ( Accepts the text that follows - subject to two )
                  ( halt conditions: C/L characters or encountering )
                  ( CR - into the nth line )
   R
; <Return> OK

: I               ( n --- inserts text into the screen buffer that )
                  ( was initially held in PAD.  All lines that )
                  ( follow line n are shifted towards the bottom )
                  ( and the last is lost )
  DUP S           ( Blanks the nth line )
  R               ( Copies the contents of PAD in the nth line )
; <Return> OK
```

The following words operate on whole screens.

```
: CLEAR           ( n --- erases the nth screen, blanking all its )
                  ( lines )
    SCR  !        ( Updates SCR )
    10   0 DO
    FORTH I       ( Transfer to FORTH to obtain the correct defi-)
                  ( nition of I which gives the current loop index )
    EDITOR E      ( Erasure of the line )
    LOOP
; <Return> OK
```

```
: COPY            ( n1 n2 --- copies screen n1 on to screen n2 )
     B/SCR *      ( First block corresponding to screen n2 )
     OFFSET @ +   ( Physical address on disk )
     SWAP         ( Addr n1 --- )
     B/SCR *      ( First block corresponding to screen n1 )
     B/SCR OVER   ( Addr block2 block2+1 --- )
     SWAP         ( Addr(n2) end(n1)+1 begin(n1)+1 --- )
     DO           ( Addr(n2) --- )
     DUP          ( Addr(n2) addr(n2) )
     FORTH I      ( Addr(n2) addr(n2) addr-current(n1) )
     BLOCK        ( Loads the current block of screen n1 in the disk )
                  ( buffer and displays its address )
     2-  !        ( Gives it as its number the number of the current )
                  ( block in screen n2 )
     1+           ( Moves on to the next block in screen n2 )
     UPDATE       ( Signals alteration of the block )
     LOOP
     DROP
     FLUSH        ( Updates on to disk all the amended blocks )
; <Return> OK
```

All the words presented above together go to make up a small line/page editor, in the sense that the basic object that can be modified is the line of text.

The words that we shall now examine allow us to work with the line itself at the character string level.

The variable R# contains a cursor pointing to the next character that can be reached by the string editor.

The first two words to be defined are the ones that enable a string to be found in a section of text, with the cursor moving as required.

```
: -TEXT           ( Addr1 n addr2 --- f if the string beginning at )
                  ( addr1 and addr2 coincide on the first n charac- )
                  ( ters, display a True flag, otherwise display a )
                  ( False flag )
   SWAP           ( Addr1 addr2 n --- )
   -DUP IF        ( If n is zero, abandon procedure )
   OVER + SWAP    ( Addr1 addr2+n addr2 --- )
   DO             ( Addr1 --- )
   DUP C@         ( Addr1 c --- )
   FORTH I C@ -   ( Addr1 c-c' --- )
   IF 0= LEAVE    ( If they are different, leave loop )
   ELSE 1+        ( If not, continue comparison )
   THEN
   LOOP
   ELSE DROP 0=
   THEN
; <Return> OK

: MATCH           ( Addr1 n1 addr2 n2 --- f n3 )
   >R >R 2DUP     ( Duplicates addr1 and n1 )
   R> R> 2SWAP    ( Addr1 n1 addr2 n2 addr1 n1 --- )
   OVER + SWAP    ( Addr1 n1 addr2 n2 addr1+n1 addr1 --- )
   DO             ( Addr1 n1 addr2 n2 --- )
   2DUP           ( Addr1 n1 addr2 n2 addr2 n2 --- )
   FORTH I        ( Addr1 n1 addr2 n2 addr2 n2 I --- )
   -TEXT          ( Do text (2) and text (1)  correspond on the n2 )
```

```
                  ( first characters? )
    IF            ( Addr1 n1 addr2 n2 --- )
    >R 2DROP R>   ( Addr1 n2 --- )
    - I SWAP -    ( n3 --- )
    0 SWAP        ( 0 n3 --- )
    0 0 LEAVE     ( Leave loop with two trailing blanks )
    THEN
    LOOP
    2DROP         ( Clear the stack )
    SWAP 0= SWAP  ( Set flag in correct direction )
; <Return> OK
```

We can now describe the first words for manipulating the line itself.

```
: TOP             ( Positions the cursor on the first character of )
                  ( the first line of the current screen )
   0 R# !
; <Return> OK

: #LOCATE         ( --- n1 n2 beginning at the current position of )
                  ( the cursor, calculates the line number and )
                  ( cursor offset in relation to the beginning of )
                  ( the line )
   R# @
   C/L  /MOD
; <Return> OK

: #LEAD           ( --- addr n beginning at the current position of )
                  ( the cursor, calculates the address addr of the )
                  ( line in the screen buffer and the offset in re- )
                  ( lation to the beginning of the line )
   #LOCATE
   LINE
   SWAP
; <Return> OK

: #LAG            ( --- addr n beginning at the current position of )
                  ( the cursor, calculates the address of the line )
                  ( in the screen buffer and the offset in relation )
                  ( to the end of the line )
   #LEAD          ( Parameters in relation to the beginning of the )
                  ( line )
   DUP  >R        ( Saves the offset )
   + C/L R> -
; <Return> OK

: M               ( n --- advances cursor n characters.  Displays )
                  ( line, including cursor, for modifications )
  R# +!           ( Moves cursor )
  CR SPACE        ( New line )
  #LEAD TYPE      ( Displays text preceding cursor )
  5F EMIT         ( Displays cursor '↑' )
  #LAG TYPE       ( Displays text following cursor )
  #LOCATE .       ( Displays the line number )
  DROP
; <Return> OK
```

```
 : T                 ( n --- displays the contents of the nth line and )
                     ( makes a copy of it in PAD )
    DUP C/L *        ( Calculates the offset of the nth line in the )
                     ( screen )
    R#  !            ( Makes the cursor point to the beginning of the )
                     ( nth line )
    H                ( Copies the nth line in PAD )
    0  M             ( Prints out the nth line on the output peripheral )
 ; <Return> OK

 : L                 ( Displays entire contents of the screen being )
                     ( modified )
    SCR @ LIST       ( Lists the current screen )
    0  M             ( Displays the line containing the cursor )
 ; <Return> OK

 : 1LINE             ( --- f searches in the current line for a string )
                     ( stored in PAD, beginning at the current cursor )
                     ( position )
   #LAG PAD COUNT    ( Prepares the parameters for MATCH )
     MATCH R# +!
 ; <Return> OK

: FIND               ( T searches the entire screen for a string held )
                     ( in PAD.  Displays an error message if checked, )
                     ( otherwise repositions cursor )
    BEGIN
    3FF R# @ <       ( Tests cursor in relation to 1023 )
    IF               ( to find out if it lies outside the screen )
    TOP              ( Top left of screen )
    PAD HERE C/L 1+  ( Moves string to HERE to display it in the error )
      CMOVE            ( message )
    0 ERROR
    THEN
    1LINE            ( Searches in the line )
    UNTIL
 ; <Return> OK


: DELETE             ( n --- deletes n characters from the cursor )
                     ( position and reassembles the line )
    >R               ( Saves the number of characters to be deleted )
    #LAG +           ( End of line )
    FORTH R -        ( R copies the top of the return stack )
    #LAG
    R MINUS R# +!    ( Moves cursor back n characters )
    #LEAD +          ( New cursor position )
    SWAP CMOVE       ( Moves the rest of the line for the deletion )
    R> BLANKS        ( Puts blanks in the empty spaces )
    UPDATE           ( Updates buffer )
; <Return> OK

: N                  ( Finds the next occurrence of a string held in )
                     ( PAD )
   FIND              ( Searches )
   0  M              ( Displays line if string found )
; <Return> OK
```

```
: F                 ( Finds the first occurrence of the string that )
                    ( follows in the input stream )
   1  TEXT
   N
; <Return> OK

: B                 ( Moves the cursor to the beginning of the )
                    ( string that matches a given string )
   PAD C@           ( Displays the length of the string contained in )
                    ( PAD )
   MINUS  M         ( Moves back cursor and redisplays line )
; <Return> OK

: X                 ( Deletes the text that follows in the input )
                    ( stream )
   1 TEXT           ( Relocation in PAD )
   FIND             ( Searches screen )
   PAD  C@          ( Length of string to be deleted )
   DELETE           ( Deletes )
   0  M             ( Displays )
; <Return> OK

: TILL              ( Deletes all characters after the current )
                    ( cursor position up to and including the first )
                    ( occurrence of the text that follows it in the )
                    ( input stream )
   #LEAD  +         ( Current cursor address )
   1  TEXT          ( Relocation in PAD )
   1LINE            ( Search in line )
   0= 0 ?ERROR      ( Error if item does not exist )
   #LEAD + SWAP -   ( Prepares the parameters for DELETE )
   DELETE
   0  M
; <Return> OK

: C                          ( Insertion, into text at current )
                             ( cursor position, of characters that )
                             ( follow in the input stream.  Characters )
                             ( that extend beyond the line length are )
                             ( lost )
  1 TEXT PAD COUNT           ( Relocation in PAD )
  #LAG ROT OVER MIN >R       ( Save MIN(nb-car, pos- cursor )
  FORTH R                    ( Copy of the return stack )
  R#  +!                     ( Repositions cursor )
  R  -  >R                   ( Number of characters to be saved )
  DUP HERE R CMOVE           ( Temporary displacement to HERE )
  HERE #LEAD + R> CMOVE      ( Restores text )
     R> CMOVE                ( Replaces string )
     UPDATE
     0  M
; <Return> OK
FORTH DEFINITIONS DECIMAL
```

Appendix 3: Solutions to Exercises

Chapter 2

```
2.1  a)  ( --- ) The stack is empty.
     b)  ( 23 33 54 --- )
     c)  ( 32 15 --- )
     d)  ( 13 15 18 --- )

2.2  a)  ab+cd+*
     b)  ab+c/de+f*+
     c)  abc+/de+ac/*/
     d)  abc/*da+bcd+/*+
```

Chapter 3

```
3.1  a)  (2 3 1 --- )
     b)  ( 2 5 --- )
     c)  ( 6 --- )
     d)  ( -20 --- )
     e)  Error: stack empty
     f)  ( 1 2 3 - 1 3 - 1 --- )

3.2  a)  : EX02A OVER + SWAP 2SWAP ROT ROT + * SWAP / ;
     b)  : EX02B >R >R ROT OVER + ROT R> + OVER *
               R> SWAP OVER / ROT 2SWAP + * SWAP / ;
     c)  : EX02C 2DUP + >R ROT DUP >R + R> OVER * R>
               2SWAP * +SWAP / ;

3.3  a)  : MINIMUM                ( addr n ... min )
             32767
             0 DO
                OVER @
                MIN
                SWAP 2+ SWAP
             LOOP
             SWAP DROP
         ;
     b) : MAXIMUM                 ( addr n ... max )
           -32768 SWAP
            0 DO
               OVER
               MAX
               SWAP 2+ SWAP
            LOOP
            SWAP DROP
         ;

3.4  a)  : SUBTRACTION MINUS + ;
     b)  : U*/MOD >R U* R> U/ ;
```

3.5 a)
```
: 0FILL
     0 DO
        0 OVER
        !
        2+
     LOOP
     DROP
;
```
b)
```
: +1FILL
   0 DO
      1 OVER
      +!
      2+
   LOOP
   DROP
;
```

3.6 a) To solve this exercise we shall use the Euclid theorem, written as follows.
To calculate the GCD of numbers a and b. First

$$a = b.q + r \text{ (integer division)}$$

We know that r is less than b. We can therefore write

$$b = r.q1 + r1$$

and similarly, until we obtain

$$r_{n-1} = r_n q_{n+1} + r_{n+1}$$

with

$$r_{n+1} = 0$$

We then know that the GCD is r_n.

```
: GCD
  SMUDGE
  DUP IF
       SWAP OVER
       /MOD DROP
       GCD
       ELSE
        DROP
       THEN
  SMUDGE ;
```

b) To calculate LCM we can use the following result

```
A * B = GCD(A,B) * LCM(A,B)
```

```
3.7  : DIV1
         DUP  >R /MOD
         0
         R> OVER
         IF
           46 EMIT
           4  0 DO SWAP 10 *
                   OVER /MOD
                   48 + EMIT
                   DUP 0= IF LEAVE THEN
                   SWAP
                   LOOP
         THEN
         DROP DROP
     ; <Return> OK

3.8  : DIV2
        DUP  >R
        /MOD 0 .R
        DUP IF
              46 EMIT
              0  SWAP
              BEGIN
                10 * R /MOD
                48 + EMIT
                SWAP 1+ SWAP
                OVER 4 =
                OVER 0= OR
              UNTIL
              DROP
            THEN
        DROP R> DROP
     ; <Return> OK

3.9  : DIV3
       DUP >R
       /MOD 0 .R
       DUP IF
             46 EMIT
             0  SWAP
             BEGIN
               OVER 4 <
               OVER *
             WHILE
               10 * R /MOD
               48 + EMIT
               SWAP 1+ SWAP
             REPEAT
             DROP
           THEN
       DROP R> DROP
     ; <Return> OK
```

3.10
```
: CONV                  ( n --- )
    16 0 DO
      15 I - 2          ( n 15-I2 --- )
      SWAP POWER        ( n 2power(15-I) --- )
      OVER AND          ( n flag --- )
      0= 0=             ( normalisation flag )
      48 + EMIT         ( n --- )
    LOOP
    DROP
; <Return> OK
```

The word POWER can be defined as follows

```
: POWER                 ( a b --- a power(b) )
    DUP  0=
    IF
        DROP DROP 1 ( 1 --- )
        ELSE
        1 SWAP          ( a 1 b --- )
        0 DO            ( a 1 --- )
         OVER  *        ( a a power(1) --- )
        LOOP            ( a a power(b) --- )
        SWAP DROP       ( a power(b) --- )
    THEN
; <Return> OK
```

3.11 For this exercise we shall use the method of Eratosthenes' sieve. This requires the construction of a vector containing all the numbers from 1 to 100. We work through this table from 1 to 100. When we find a valid number, it is extracted and made the first entity, and all its multiples in the vector are rendered invalid. Here the method of invalidation is to replace the value with 0. In our vector, we shall store the values in one byte.

```
0 VARIABLE ERATOS 98 ALLOT
        : SET           ( Pfa(ERATOS) --- )
          101 1 DO
             I OVER C!  ( Addr --- )
             1+
          LOOP
          DROP
        ; <Return> OK
```

We now construct the word N-MUL that will invalidate all the multiples of n that occur in ERATOS.

```
: N-MUL                         ( n --- )
      101 OVER                  ( n 101 n --- )
      DO
         I 1 - ERATOS           ( n i-1 addr --- )
         +                      ( n addr (i) --- )
         0 SWAP C!              ( n --- )
         DUP
      +LOOP
      DROP
; <Return> OK
```

```
: PRIME                         ( --- )
  ERATOS SET                    ( addr --- )
     ERATOS  1  .
     101 2 DO
        I 1 -                   ( addri-1 --- )
        OVER + C@               ( addr n --- )
        DUP IF
           DUP . N-MUL          ( addr --- )
        ELSE
           DROP                 ( addr --- )
        THEN
     LOOP
     DROP                       ( --- )
; <Return> OK
```

3.12 First we define three variables to hold the counts of vowels, consonants and spaces.

```
0 VARIABLE VOW
0 VARIABLE CON
0 VARIABLE SPC
```

Then we define words to test whether a character is a space or a vowel.

```
: ?SPACE
     BL =
; <Return> OK

: ?VOWEL
    DUP  65 =
    OVER 69 = OR
    OVER 73 = OR
    OVER 79 = OR
    SWAP 85 = OR
; <Return> OK
```

We can now define ANALYSE. It assumes that a character which is not a space or a vowel must be a consonant.

```
: ANALYSE
    0  VOW ! 0  CON ! 0  SPC !
    34 WORD
    HERE COUNT 0
    DO DUP I + C@
       DUP ?VOWEL
       IF 1 VOW +!
       ELSE DUP ?SPACE
            IF 1 SPC +!
            ELSE 1 CON +!
            THEN
       THEN DROP
    LOOP DROP
    CR SPC? ." SPACES"
    CR VOW? ." VOWELS"
    CR CON? ." CONSONANTS"
    CR
; <Return> OK
```

Chapter 6

```
6.1  a)  : ,            ( n --- )
            HERE !
            2 ALLOT
         ;
     b)  : C,           ( n --- )
            HERE C!
            1 ALLOT
         ;
```

6.2 The aim of the word COMPILE is to postpone compilation at the time of execution. The CFA of the word that follows COMPILE is then placed in the first free cell in the dictionary. Note also that, on execution of COMPILE, the interpretation pointer is located on the return stack.

```
: COMPILE
      R>               ( Points to the next word )
      DUP  2+ >R       ( Increments IP ) ( Addr --- )
      @ ,              ( Compiles the CFA of the word )
;
```

6.3

```
: IF                   ( Addr --- )
    COMPILE OBRANCH    ( For the branch )
    HERE               ( For calculation of the offset )
    0 ,                ( Cell reservation )
;

IMMEDIATE
: THEN                 ( Addr --- )
      HERE             ( Addr absolute branch )
      OVER -           ( Addr relative branch )
      SWAP !           ( Stores offset OBRANCH or BRANCH )
;
IMMEDIATE
: ELSE                 ( Addr --- Addr' )
      COMPILE BRANCH   ( For branch )
      HERE 0 ,         ( Addr Here --- )
      SWAP             ( Here Addr --- )
       [COMPILE] THEN  ( THEN is immediate )
;
IMMEDIATE
```

Bibliography

Bartoldi P. *Stepwise Development and Debugging Using a Small Well-Structured Interactive Language for Data Acquisition and Instrument Control*
Proceedings of the International Symposium and Course on Mini and Microcomputers and their Applications. 1976

Brodie L. *Starting FORTH*
Prentice-Hall, 1981

Decus *FORTH Programming System for the PDP-11*
DECUS, No. 11-232, September 1975

Ewing M.S. *The Caltech FORTH Manual.* 1978

Fierbach G. *FORTH the Language of Machine Independence*
Computer Design. Vol 20, No. 6. June 1981

FORTH Inc. *FORTH a Fresh Approach to Programming*
Small System Journal. Vol. 3 No. 2. 1978

FORTH Inc. *Using FORTH*
Forth Inc. 1979

de Grandis-Harrison R. *FORTH on the BBC Microcomputer*
Acornsoft, Cambridge, 1983

Haydon *All About FORTH*
Mountain View Press

Hicks S.M. *FORTH: A Cost Saving Approach to Software Development*
Wescon/Los Angeles. 1978

Hicks S.M. *FORTH's Forte is Tighter Programming*
Electronics, March 1979

Hogan T. *Discover FORTH: Learning and Programming the FORTH Language*
Osborne/McGraw-Hill, 1982

James J.S. *FORTH for Microcomputers*
Dr Dobb's Journal, May 1978

Katzan H. *Invitation to FORTH*
Petrocelli Books, 1981

Knecht K.B. *Introduction to FORTH*
H.W. Sams, 1982

Loeliger R.G. *Threaded Interpretive Languages*
Byte Books, 1981

Meyer B. *Méthodes de Programmation*
Baudouin C. (Eyrolles)

Monroe A.J. *A FORTH Floating-Point Package*
Dr Dobb's Journal, No. 71, September 1982

Moore C.H. *FORTH: A New Way to Program Mini-Computers*
Astron. Astrophys. Suppl. No. 15, 1974

Moore C.H. *The FORTH Program for Spectral Line Observing*
Rather E.D. Proc. IEEE, September 1973

Moore C.H. *The Use of FORTH in Process Control*

Rather E.D. Proc. of the International '77 Mini-Micro Computer Conference, Geneva, IPC and Technology Press, England, 1977

Moore C.H. *The Evolution of FORTH, an Unusual Language* Byte, August 1980

Odette L. *Z8000 FORTH* Dr Dobb's Journal, No. 71, September 1982

Rather E.D. *The FORTH Approach to Operating Systems*

Moore C.H. ACM '76 Proceedings

Sachs J. *An Introduction to STOIC* Technical Report BMEC TR001 Harvard-MIT Program in Health Science and Technology, June 1976

Scanlon L.J. *FORTH Programming* H.W. Sams, 1983

Stein P. *The FORTH Dimension: Mini Language has Many Faces* Computer Decisions, November 1975

Stevens W.R. *A FORTH Primer* Kitt Peak National Observatory, 1979

Taylor A. *FORTH Becoming Hothouse for Developing Languages* Computerworld, July 1979

Ting C.H. *System Guide to Fig-FORTH* Offete Enterprises Inc.

Wells D.C. *Interactive Image Analysis for Astronomers* Computer, August 1977

Winfield A. *Complete FORTH* Sigma Technical Press, 1983

Index